THE TIGER OF THE LAND OF MORNING CALM

Russian Ambassador's Thoughts on South Korea

THE TIGER OF THE LAND OF MORNING CALM

Russian Ambassador's Thoughts on South Korea

Gleb Ivashentsov

PENTAGON PRESS

The Tiger of the Land of Morning Calm:
Russian Ambassador's Thoughts on South Korea
by Gleb Ivashentsov

First Published in 2014

ISBN 978-81-8274-775-3

Published by
PENTAGON PRESS
206, Peacock Lane, Shahpur Jat,
New Delhi-110049
Phones: 011-64706243, 26491568
Telefax: 011-26490600
email: rajan@pentagonpress.in
website: www.pentagonpress.in

Branch:
Prime Arcade
Office #11
1154 Saifee Street
Opp. M.G.Road, Camp
Pune-411001
Email: pentagonpresspune@gmail.com

Printed at Avantika Printers Private Limited.

Dedicated to my wife
Irina Ivashentsova

Contents

The Other Korea: Russian Ambassador's Impressions and Thoughts About S. Korea

Gleb Ivashentsov served as the Ambassador Extraordinary and Plenipotentiary of the Russian Federation in the Republic of Korea from 2005 to 2009. His present book is the first book on South Korea ever written by a foreign ambassador stationed in Seoul. The book is a narration not traditional in its form, combining the professional memoirs of a diplomat with a vivid, friendly tale by a person of inquisitive bent on his impressions of a foreign country.

One can find here a unique perspective on the events in South Korea as well as a very personal understanding of the Korean character, which let Koreans within one generation turn their war-ravaged motherland into a prosperous, highly developed modem country.

It is with deep concern that Ambassador Ivashentsov writes on confrontation between two Korean states. That threat to Northeast Asia and global peace and security has especially sharpened in recent years due to the nuclear issue on the Korean Peninsula. He emphasizes that "settlement of the nuclear issue of the Korean Peninsula and inter-Korean normalization are two wheels of the same cart, of the only cart that could carry us to our common destination of a system of peace and security in Northeast Asia."

For Ambassador Ivashentsov, Russia's foreign policy in the East has a triune goal which is *to* protect the country's national interests and security in the Asia-Pacific, to use economic and political potential in the Asia-Pacific for an advance of the Russian economy, and to give priority to the development of Eastern Siberia and the Russian Far Eastern regions, raising living standards of their people.

The author's logic is straight that "Russia could maintain security at her Far Eastern frontiers only through getting her neighbors interested in advantages of long-term and wide-scale economic partnership."

Therefore, in his opinion, Russia's task in interacting with the Republic of Korea is not just to work out checks and balances of the system of multilateral security in Northeast Asia. Russia needs the ROK for trade and as a partner in the economic development of Siberia and the Far Eastern regions.

Sir Henry Wotton, the British envoy to Venice in the 17th century, wrote that "An ambassador is an honest man sent to lie abroad for the good of his country." Those who dealt with Amb. Ivashentsov in Korea know that he never lied to his partners. That made it possible for him to do a lot for the good of both Russia and the Republic of Korea, strengthening their bilateral partnership in so many spheres, from culture to energy and the joint space flight.

From 'Diplomacy' magazine of Seoul

Introduction

"What is it like there, beyond the dragon's teeth of the 38th parallel?" an old friend asked me when I came to Moscow on my first vacation from my posting in Seoul.

This joking question nonetheless reflected quite accurately the perception of Korea that was dominant back in the 1960s among the students of Moscow State Institute of International Relations (MGIMO), future staff members of the Ministry of Foreign Affairs, and of other departments engaged both in international relations and in foreign trade. After the Korean War of 1950-53, the 38th parallel separated the two confrontational Korean states. One of them was the Democratic People's Republic of Korea where the Korean people led by the Labor Party of Korea and its leader comrade Kim Il Sung were moving successfully toward building socialism with comprehensive aid from the Soviet Union. The other was South Korea, closed for the Soviet citizens, with people living in abject poverty, deprived of any rights, oppressed by the puppet regimes first of Syng Man Rhee and then of Park Chung-hee, surviving with the military help of the American imperialists.

Today, forty five years after graduation, I look back at those Soviet opinions of the situation in Korea, and I have to say there was quite a lot of truth to them. By the late 1960s, the DPRK achieved significant successes in economy and in its social programs, it rebuilt its industry and agriculture destroyed by the war, and its economic development was progressing faster than in South Korea. And no historian, whether South Korean, American, or Russian, would dispute the fact that Syng Man Rhee's regime was dictatorial, corrupt, and pro-American. At the time of his resignation, South Korea's per capita GDP was less than the GDP of Papua New Guinea and Nigeria, famine was not infrequent in villages, cities experienced regular blackouts. When general Park Chung-hee came to power in 1961 as a result of a military coup d'état, people prosecuted for political reasons were sentenced to death, any assemblies were prohibited, and the mass media were under total control.

In 2005, I came to an entirely different country with a developed civil society, the country of the "Korean economic miracle," whose movies and athletes gained world renown. However, the 38th parallel still divided Korea, and it was not merely demarcated with dragon's teeth, it had two extremely powerful armies in a stand-off with state-of-the-art weapons. North Korea conducted nuclear and missile tests and thus exacerbated the situation even more.

In my book, I won't dwell on North Korea, I won't discuss what their leaders did wrong and why. I think it would be a task better suited for those who worked in Pyongyang which I unfortunately have never visited.

I will speak about my personal impressions of South Korea where I worked for four years (2005-2009) as the Ambassador of the Russian Federation. I will speak about some Korean experiences Russia and other countries could use; I will speak about people I met in Seoul, about how I envision further developments in the Far East and what Russia's policy in the region should be. I hope it will be interesting and maybe useful for some people.

I express my gratitude to all friends who helped me with this book, especially Aleksandr Zubko.

1

A Few Words about Myself and My Life

My life has been tied to the diplomatic services for over half a century, ever since the summer of 1962 when I became a student of Moscow State Institute of International Relations of the USSR Ministry of Foreign Affairs.

There have never before been any diplomats in my family. The men in the Ivashentsov family hailed from the Vologda and Kostroma regions; I can trace my lineage to the 16th century. My ancestors mostly served in the military; they took part in the Seven Years' War of 1756-65, in the War of 1812, in the Crimean war of 1854-55, and in many other Russian military campaigns.

In the late 19th century, they shed their military uniform and assumed a civil one, although they still loved weapons. One of my forebears, A.P. Ivashentsov, was mentioned in a recently published book *One Hundred Great Russian Hunters.* He developed several models of hunting guns manufactured in Tula and Izhevsk up until the late 1930s, and his books on hunting and hunting weapons are still in print and in demand. My grandfather G.A. Ivashentsov was a doctor, and my father A.G.

Ivashentsov was a geologist. Each of them plied their trade honest and hard for the benefit of their homeland.

Since childhood, I enjoyed learning languages; I studied German at school and English with a private tutor; my paternal grandmother who spoke German, French, and English, believed that knowledge of a foreign language befits every educated person regardless of his or her professional occupation. My parents were both geologists and, naturally, they wanted me to follow in their footsteps. Already as a child, I went on geological expeditions with them, and when I finished the 9th grade at the age of 16, they sent me to an expedition on my own. Yet I decided to apply to Moscow State Institute of International Relations (MGIMO); its graduates worked in the Ministry of Foreign Affairs and in the Ministry of Foreign Trade. I was accepted at my first attempt, without my parents' calling in any favors. Only after I was admitted my mother actually asked where the institute was located because she wanted to go there to see with her own eyes the list of admitted applicants posted by the entrance and my name on that list.

Studying at MGIMO

Teaching in MGIMO was good. Our professors were knowledgeable and experienced, and I still remember them with great respect. I was placed in the Hindi language group, much to my joy. India was then very popular in the Soviet Union, and personally, I was fascinated by Jawaharlal Nehru who looked very much like my grandfather the doctor.

The Orient determined my subsequent work and my professional circles, and I never regretted that. Studying Oriental languages makes one diligent and patient since learning an Oriental language requires no less than three hours of work a day. It broadens your horizons because you also discover a new civilization, that of India, China, the Arabs; none of that happens when studying English or French. And those of us who learned Oriental languages did study a western language, too, either English or French. It's worth noting that, as a rule, "Orientalists" were also excellent at their western languages. Several leading English interpreters at the Ministry of Foreign Affairs started out as "Orientalists."

Going Over the Top with Ideology

One thing that was annoying during my university years was going over the top with ideological subjects. Those who persisted in imposing these subjects on students must have believed that they would educate the best "ideology foot soldiers." Yet in practice, they achieved just the opposite, as we saw clearly at the turn of 1980s-1990s. People who waged the fiercest attacks against "the communist past" were the very same people who had defended dissertations on dialectic materialism and scientific communism, people who had taught these subjects for years.

I have always been repelled by falsity, and we were inundated with fake pledges of "allegiance to Leninism," with proclamations of the necessity to "draw our strength from Lenin's legacy," etc. I remember being quite taken aback when at some meeting, a person I greatly respected, a former Ambassador to India, suddenly burst into a fit of fake revelations about "seeking an evening advice from our dear comrade Lenin." "Sometimes a difficult question plagues you," he prated, "you don't know what to do. And then you take a volume of Lenin's works, leaf through it, and there it is, your answer."

Those who intend to become career diplomats need practical skills, not theoretical knowledge. I will explain what I mean. In Russia, we have this TV show called "Brainiacs." Participants compete answering questions in history and geography, and the winners are admitted to MGIMO. I like these kids, I can see they know a lot from a whole range of subjects. But the knowledge itself doesn't mean they have analytical capabilities, it doesn't mean they are fit to become diplomats. And let's call a spade a spade, the show participants aren't so much brainiacs as they are walking databases. But the Internet provides a lot more information today. As Ambassador, I have very little use of a staff member who can list all the feats of Heracles or all the Pacific island mini-states, if that very same staff member cannot tactfully get rid of an unwanted visitor, cannot promptly find the documents on customs statistics, or determine the guest parking order for an embassy reception.

When talking about professional suitability, I always think about an episode from a novel by Sydney Sheldon who was very popular in 1970s. The heroine comes to the office of some New York lawyer; she wants the job of a secretary that has been advertised. In the office, she sees about twenty other applicants. Some of them are beautiful, and she grows fearful. Suddenly, the lawyer's assistant runs out of the inner office and screams into space: "Where am I going to find that issue of Newsweek from two months back?" Our girl doesn't say a word, she just goes downstairs to a beauty salon; she knows beauty salons always have some out-of-date magazines, and she brings the lawyer's assistant the issue he so desperately needs. She is hired immediately. When admitting applicants, we should look not for factual knowledge, but for abilities to compare the facts, analyze them, in other words, we should look for an ability to think and to find ways out of unusual predicaments.

At the MGIMO School of International Economic Relations, they like to tell an old story which happened back when it was the Institute of Foreign Trade. Anastas Mikoyan himself, a member of the highest governing bodies of the USSR for over forty years, and the-then minister of foreign trade, came to the final exam on monetary and financial operations. One of the A-students was answering. He got a very simple question: "Promissory notes." He started with complete self-confidence, "A promissory note is a strictly defined document which certifies the obligations of its issuer... Promissory notes are transferred by endorsement..." "Now that's great," Mikoyan smiled and then said with his typical Armenian accent, "I see that you know all that. Now do kindly write a promissory note for me." And here this A-student got, as it were, mud on his face. Turned out, he had never in his entire life seen a single promissory note so he could not write one. Naturally, after such a screw-up in front on the minister himself he was left without his *summa cum laude*. In all the MGIMO Schools, students should be taught in such a way that they don't find themselves in such situations. Unfortunately, it does happen all the time.

On Korean Studies Specialists and on Other Matters, Too

Historically, Oriental studies have always been Russians' forte. As far back as 1720, Peter I issued a decree on the Collegium of Foreign Affairs which included "department of Turkish and other Oriental languages." Expanding South and East, Russia took care to train professionals and experts to set up relations with neighboring countries. Russia's Turkic studies, Iranian studies, Afghan studies, Indian studies, and Chinese studies achieved world renown.

Here is one telltale example. An eminent Pakistani diplomat in charge of Islamabad's Afghan policies after the USSR moved into Afghanistan once told me that he had all Soviet publications on Afghanistan summarized and then partially translated. He was amazed by the scope of it, whatever piece of information you needed, be it, for instance, information on Afghan tribes contained therein, and by the depth and insight of the analysis.

He admitted that in his estimation, pre-revolutionary Russian and subsequent Soviet research on Afghanistan was of better academic quality than research not only of Pakistani, but also of British scholars.

Trouble was, Soviet political decision-makers rarely conferred with scholars, and Afghanistan is a case in point.

On the other hand, there were scholars who were after honors and prestigious positions, and they weren't so much engaged in research, as they were engaged in tailoring their articles and books to the pronouncements of the most recent Communist Party Congress. The 1960s-1970s saw a proliferation of works on the countries of Asia and Africa where the authors repeated the unrealistic mantras about the non-capitalist development path for former colonies and about the "national democracy" states in the "third world."

Learning by rote has always plagued social sciences in the USSR. I remember taking my candidate of sciences degree qualifying examination in philosophy in the 1970s. I was a graduate student in a prestigious academic institution. One of the questions was succinct: "Anticommunism." I prepared a detailed answer, starting with the theory of totalitarianism. I mentioned Hannah Arendt, Martin Heidegger, and suddenly the examiner from the Institute of Philosophy of the USSR Academy of Sciences interrupted me, "Why are you telling us all that?" Turned out, I was supposed to give a rote answer, "The party documents of the CPSU and its fraternal parties delineate the crucial tendencies in the struggle against anticommunism, anti-Sovietism, and about a dozen other –isms, including Maoism and Zionism."

Korean studies wasn't an exception. We have always had and still have wonderful scholars of Korean language, culture, and history. As regards experts on the current state of affairs, for decades after the World War II, their take on the situation was openly biased. They only looked at North Korea, and saw only its good sides, although largely, I believe, they were quite sincere in their views. And South Korea was for them a kind of a land on the other side of the looking glass.

When South Korea was "discovered" at the turn of 1980s-1990s, many Korean studies specialists saw only the good things there, and they started publishing works claiming the opposite of what they had been saying just a few years prior. Russian specialists in Korean studies working in international relations are usually people with a good command of Korean and with a good knowledge of life in the country. Their principal trouble lies in the fact once an Orientalist with a rare language gets inside the system of the Russian Ministry of Foreign Affairs, he is usually "chained for life" to the country of the language he knows. It is true about the specialists in Chinese, Japanese, Vietnamese studies etc. I happen to know a person who spent his entire diplomatic career in the same smallish Asian country, rising in rank from an attaché to the ambassador. Only shortly before retirement, he was posted to another country, although still in the same region.

I believe that having people spend decades in the same country is highly counterproductive. They have no opportunities for professional development, they develop blind spots, they see everything in the light of their previous experience, they are unable to notice new developments and trends. Besides, they develop what Americans call "localitis," when a person assumes the point of view and the attitudes of the locals of the country where he is posted.

I had a chance to observe a tell-tale example. South Korea was holding local elections expected to have significant influence on the overall situation in the country. I asked the Embassy's leading Korean studies specialist to prepare a report that could serve as a basis for my report to Moscow. The staff member brought me a very detailed report on the elections' progress, explaining why the elections in a particular region were carried by Park from party X and not by Choi from party Y, what the differences between the parties were, who defected from one faction to another, who had bribed whom and where it had happened, and where smear campaigns had proven effective. The report failed to address one point only: it contained absolutely nothing on the significance of the election results for the future of the Russian-Korean relations.

Knowing the language of the country of your posting is important for a diplomat, but it is not the most important thing. It is far more important for the diplomat to be the kind of person whom the local figures would find interesting to deal with. People will share their thoughts with you only if you are capable of appreciating other people's thoughts, if you can produce something interesting, and not just routing gushing on the beauties of the country or the stories of what people eat in Russia while drinking vodka. Today, it's traditional to criticize Soviet appointments of high ranking Communist Party officials as Ambassadors. It is now traditional to deride them as former secretaries of regional or republican party committees with utterly no understanding of diplomacy. Yet their tenures proved that being masters of power play, having gone through the hard school of party work and having accumulated a great and diverse life experience, they had a better understanding of diplomacy than career diplomats from the Moscow Ministry who only exceled in preparing reports for their bosses. Those who worked in India about forty-forty five years ago, remember the great respect with which Indira Gandhi treated Soviet ambassadors I. A. Benediktov and N. M. Pegov. They had not been career diplomats, but they had been wise men with a large experience of state governance.

How to Show a Brazen Foreigner his Proper Place

When you work abroad, you meet some nice and welcoming people, but you also meet some open or covert ill-wishers who seize every chance to land someone in trouble at public functions or slander your country in the media.

I remember a story in Delhi 1980, after the Soviet troops had been deployed in Afghanistan. Our Embassy held a reception on occasion of the Soviet Army Day, February 23. It was the last reception of this kind attended by military attachés from NATO countries. They never attended such receptions until the USSR's withdrawal from Afghanistan. US military attachés turned out in full force, they must have known it was their last chance to have some vodka and caviar. We had a crowd of ruddy-cheeked guys in uniforms with aglets, some awkward gals in uniform, with side caps, etc.

Our Embassy had some MGIMO interns then. And the owner of some particularly impressive aglets attached himself to one of those interns. And a short distance away from them, an embassy counselor was engrossed in a conversation with some guest or other. That counselor had, as people sometime gently put it, certain additional departmental affiliation. Naturally, this affiliation wasn't openly acknowledged but everyone, including Americans, knew about it, just as we knew our counselor's counterparts in the American embassy. While talking to our intern, this agletted guy starts pointing his finger at our embassy counselor and asks in a deliberately loud voice, "And who is this gentleman? Who is this gentleman?" Our intern should have given a simple answer, "This Mr. N., a Counselor of our Embassy," but he became embarrassed, and that just egged the American on. I could see that the situation called for my intervention. I come up to them and introduce myself and ask the American who he might be. He tells me very ponderously, "I am Assistant Naval

Attaché for the Air," and of course he's referring to the US Air Force. But the first meaning of the word "air" refers to the air we breathe. So I address him with the air of a person who has trouble understanding spoken English, "Oh, attaché for the air... so you mean to tell me you break wind to fill the sails of the American navy?" Everybody around, including American military gals with their side caps, burst into laughter. The agletted guy chose to quietly merge with the crowd.

The second story happened in Myanmar. I traveled around the country in the company of other ambassadors. It was a long bus journey, we were quite exhausted, and to cheer up, we started telling funny stories. My English colleague had been previously posted to Poland, and he had picked up a few jokes that weren't just anti-Soviet, they were plain Russophobic. And he decided to share them. Mostly his jokes had to do with the KGB. I had to respond. I did it with a limerick of a rather bawdy nature, suitable for an all-male company only, and told the story of an Englishman who could never "rise to the occasion" and therefore could not compete with Russians from the aforementioned service. Everybody had a good laugh, and the Englishman never told any more jokes about Russians, be those jokes Polish or otherwise.

And here is a story that happened in Seoul. When I was posted there, Seoul had about a hundred of embassies. Moreover, about 30 ambassadors were accredited to the nearby cities of Beijing and Tokyo. Those ambassadors also visited Seoul to attend various functions held for the entire diplomatic corps such as the annual Presidential reception, the celebration of the Foundation of Korea (October 3), or the parade celebrating the Liberation Day (August 15).

Ambassadors to Seoul might not have treated each other with sincere warmth, but at least they were respectful and proper. Naturally, there were disagreements, frictions, conflicts between states; ambassadors, however, adhered to a certain ethics: if you are accredited to the Republic of Korea, you should mind your business which is your state's relations with Korea and not make public jabs at third countries which you or your country's leaders happen to dislike for some reason.

But of course there is always someone who wants to make a splash, even if it means turning himself into a laughingstock. The Polish Ambassador did just that in Seoul.

We had another round of the six-Party talks on the nuclear issue of the Korean Peninsula (NIKP), with the participation of two Koreas, China, Russia, the US, and Japan. The newly-arrived Polish ambassador paid me a protocol visit and inquired about my take on the prospects of resolving the issue. He was all smiles, he spoke good Russian, he left a favorable impression, and I detailed to him my views on the subject, and I also emphasized that the solution would be effective only if the interests of all the parties concerned were taken into account. I also mentioned the need for flexibility and for finding a compromise.

A few days later, a prominent Seoul newspaper published an interview the Polish ambassador had given in English to a journalist I happened to know quite well. He was interviewed on account of his posting to Seoul. He briefly touched upon the issues of Polish-Korean trade which went on much as usual, and then he spent three quarters of his interview talking about the Russian threat to Poland. He claimed that Russia trained thousands of missiles on Poland, and consequently, Poland could do one thing only: allow the US to deploy an National Missile Defense (NMD) site. He strongly advised that Koreans not listen to Russians because whatever Russians say about mutually acceptable solutions to anything, be it the nuclear issue of the Korean Peninsula or anything else, it is nothing but smokescreen used to lull the intended victims of Russia's planned aggression. In other words, my Korean friends, do as we, Poles, do, hide under the American umbrella, avoid all those six-party talks where Russians are involved, and while you are at it, tell those Russians to take a hike.

I decided to respond via the same newspaper, especially since I was on good terms with its owner. Next day, the paper published my "letter to the editor." I thanked the Polish ambassador for explaining the reasons the US had decided to deploy an NMD site in Poland. I said that no efforts had been spared to convince both Russia and our partners in the EU that the NMD was intended to protect Europe and the US from missile strikes by such rogue states as Iran and North Korea. And here is my Polish colleague claiming that the American NMD is intended to protect Poland from the "thousands of Russian missiles" trained on it. I inquired where he had received the information about those missiles from, I had never encountered such data anywhere. I expressed hope that I would hear what the US and other NATO countries have to say about the Polish ambassador's interpretation of the NMD. I also touched upon the six-party talks and stated with particular emphasis that no international agreement could ever be achieved without a compromise, and therefore statements like that of the Polish Ambassador are particularly pernicious as the six parties involved (Poland not being one of them) spare no efforts trying to resolve an issue that poses a grave threat to both regional and global security.

My response to the Polish ambassador met with a lot of interest in the diplomatic corps and in the South Korean Ministry for Foreign Affairs. The splash it made was all the greater because for reasons unknown to me the newspaper published it in two issues in two different sections. People laughed at the Polish ambassador openly. I think the Americans must have given him a piece of their mind for his irresponsible prattle. He ended up writing a penitent letter to me claiming he had never made any anti-Russian statements to the press and the Korean journalist had invented everything. Needless to say, Korean journalists didn't exactly lavish their attention on the Polish ambassador afterwards.

An Ambassador's Wife

An ambassador's wife plays a huge part in his life. I think an ambassador without a wife isn't really up to scratch, although there are certainly some exceptions. And it's not only because, as the poet put it, "At night, you want to wrap your clamor in something feminine, gentle."[1] Naturally, after a long day full of cares and troubles, it is important to come home to a warm and cheering welcome. Yet it is even more important to stay in shape, both physically and mentally.

An ambassador, just like any other person in charge, is very lonely. Maybe even more lonely than other people. In Russia, a person in charge can always visit his or her friends or relatives to share the troubles, to relieve the soul, and they will understand and maybe give advice depending on their situation and experience.

An ambassador has no such recourse. His closest friends may be hundreds, even thousands kilometers away. And sharing one's troubles with someone in the embassy is out of the question. Whatever you share of your thoughts or doubts will be common knowledge in the embassy sooner or later. And when you are in charge, the people around you should always see you as a confident, single-minded leader who knows no doubt. That is the only way of ensuring that people will carry out your orders, not because you are in charge but because you are a person they believe.

1. Vladimir Mayakovsky, *Cloud in Trousers.* // Backbone Flute: Selected Poetry of Vladimir Mayakovsky. Translated by Andrey Kneller, 2008, p. 7.

The second reason why ambassadors are so lonely is that the service demands that they spend the greater parts of their lives away from home, coming back only for brief spells of time during their vacation, with gaps of a year or more in between. And all the while, ambassadors' families live their own lives. Their children grow up, get married, start their own families, get divorced. Their elderly parents retire, fall ill, then pass away. Friends are fired due to jealousy and intrigues. Yet all of that seems to transpire in a parallel universe, you are far away, you cannot intervene in the lives of those dear to you, you learn news about their lives from their letters or from telephone conversations. My Egyptian colleague once said that diplomats are aliens in the countries where they are posted to, but sometimes, we become aliens in our homeland as well. I remember the words the brother of an ambassador said in his funereal eulogy, "For us, you haven't died. You have just been posted to a different place yet again."

Age is yet another reason for loneliness. People usually reach the rank of ambassador when they are fairly advanced in years. By that time, the numbers of your friends and relatives have already dwindled. Some are no longer part of your life, some just parted from this life altogether. You have a successful career, but alas, human nature is such that not everyone takes your success well. As a famous film director once said, success means acquiring enemies, and great success means losing friends.

A diplomat's wife, especially an ambassador's wife, should always be at his side. She is almost an army wife. She should be her husband's closest friend and most reliable advisor in all matters save the official ones, although sometimes, a female perspective helps notice certain nuances in the behavior of those locals her husband interacts with, and she can offer some tips as to how best interact with some person or other. Her personal charm, the personal acquaintances she could strike with wives of eminent local politicians, businessmen, and artists during various official functions could help expand the social circle of the ambassador and of the embassy as a whole.

When it comes to receptions, dinners, musical events held at the embassy, the ambassador's wife is second in importance after the ambassador himself. She should constantly remember that for many foreign guests, she embodies the collective image of her homeland's women, her behavior provides the basis for judging their charm, education, and attractiveness.

That's why an ambassador's wife who is boorish, who doesn't care about her appearance, uses every pretext to avoid protocol functions does a great disservice both to her husband and to the state which appointed her husband as its representative abroad.

I am also dead set against diplomats' wives working in any organizations of the host country, even teaching Russian language in local universities. The wife of a member of the embassy's personnel carries a diplomatic passport and possesses diplomatic immunity, that is, among other things, she doesn't pay taxes in the host country. Yet if she is a salaried employee at a local organization or business, she must pay taxes, otherwise a scandal is just waiting to happen.

Such a scandal befell the wife of one of the ambassadors to South Korea, the press got a whiff of it, and chewed on the subject for nearly a week. This lady made jewelry. I cannot say her works had some stunning artistic quality. They were rather large gaudy brooches made of aluminum or plastic that could be sold for ten bucks tops. Yet the embassy where the lady's husband was the ambassador was daily besieged by long lines of people applying for visas, as South Koreans thought it very prestigious to receive an education in that particular country, and local businessmen were greatly interested in doing business there.

The lady was a great businesswoman. She arranged for an

exhibition of her works in one of Seoul's prestigious art galleries. Scandalmongers claimed that potential buyers were hinted that a purchase would help them receive better treatment at the embassy.

Over a couple of days, the lady sold twenty thousand dollars worth of jewelry. And then South Korean Revenue Service learned of that business, and the story went public. The lady's fellow countrymen, many of whom taught their native language at Korean schools, were particularly indignant. They wrote enraged letters to local newspapers stating that they paid taxes from their 500-dollar salaries, and the lady whose husband made many times that amount avoided taxes. I would never want any of our diplomats to find themselves in the situation of that jewelry lady's husband.

The ambassador's wife should always set an example to all other women at the embassy both in her appearance and in her behavior. And it should be a subtle example, not an in-your-face statement, and if that example is a worthy one, she shall be imitated.

Gleb and Irina Ivashentsov

Speaking at a Korean University

Prime Minister Han Seun-soo presenting to Ambassador of Russia, Gleb A.Ivashentsov, the Khanhwa Order for distinguished diplomatic service

A model of an armored Turtle-ship Geobukson invented by Koreans in the 16-th century

Procession of Buddhists in Seoul on Buddha's birthday

A Korean table is laid

The newly weds

The orchestra at a Korean wedding

A Korean Musician

President Roh Moo-heun and his wife Kwon Yang-sook

Presentation of Credentials to President Roh Moo-heun

At lunch with Foreign Minister Ban Ki-moon (2006)

With Foreign Minister Ban Ki-moon (2006)

At Ban Ki-moon's farewell party

Irina Ivashentsova with Ban Ki-moon's wife Yoo Soon-taek

With President Lee Myung-bak

With Shin Dong-bin, Lotte Group chairman. On the right A.A.Shuruburin, Russian Trade Representative in Seoul

Russia-Korea Space crew, South Korean astronaut Yi So-yeon with Russian cosmonauts Sergei Volkov and Oleg Kononenko

With South Korean astronaut Yi So-yeon and her back-up Ko Sang

A horse made of tangerines in a street of Seoul

A symbol of aviation at Incheon International Airport

The new City Hall of Seoul

The Namdemun gate has been restored

They like this type of metal sculptures in South Korea

With Korean girls who studied in Russia

What a beautiful Matrioshka doll !

Interview to South Korean TV

At the Suwon University

A dance item from the Embassy school

Russian schoolgirls performing at the Seoul Diplomatic bazaar

What to buy from Russians? The preferences of each spouse are quite obvious

Irina Ivashentsova with Andre Kim

Korean beauties at the Parade of Nations

This is famous Korean gingseng

At Haendae Beach in Busan

With Lee Se-ung, President, Seoul Cyber University

With Ambassadors of India, Kazakhstan and US

2

Koreans

According to Korean myths, Koreans are direct descendants of a god's son and a she-bear. The myth has it that the heavenly king Hwanin let his son Hwanung and three thousand of his followers descend to Baek Mountain where Hwanung founded a divine city, established laws and started to teach people different crafts, agriculture, and medicine. Once, Hwanung happened to hear a tiger and a she-bear praying to him in a cave, asking to be turned into people. Hwanung gave them each twenty cloves of garlic and a blade of divine mugwort, told them to eat nothing else and to avoid sunlight for a hundred days. The tiger broke that injunction and left the cave, but the she-bear persevered and became a beautiful woman. Hwanung married her, and she had a son named Dangun, whom Koreans believe to be their progenitor. The day when Hwanung descended to earth in the year 2333 BC, is celebrated in the Republic of Korea on October 3 as a national holiday, the day of the foundation of the Korean state.

Koreans made the first ever metal type, built armored Turtle-ships *Geobukseon* which allowed them to route the Japanese fleet in the late 16th century, they invented Hangul, a unique writing system acclaimed as one of the best in the world in its logic, simplicity, and accessibility.

Korean attitude to life is based on the philosophy of the two linked yet opposed energies, Yin and Yang, also called the Great Principles. The state flag of the Republic of Korea is the most obvious reflection of it. It is white, its central emblem reflects the union and interaction of Yin (the blue element) and Yang (the red element). In the corners are trigrams also made up of Yin (interrupted bars) and Yang (uninterrupted bars). The trigrams signify (moving clockwise from the top part of the shaft): heaven, south, summer, and air; moon, west, fall, and water; Earth, north, winter, and earth; sun, east, spring, and fire. The color black signifies vigilance, endurance, justice, and chastity.

In the course of their history, Koreans had to repel Mongolian, Japanese, and Manchurian aggressions. On the other hand, life in the country itself went at a fairly slow pace in accordance with traditions set a long time ago. Of course, just like any other state, Korea experienced palace coups and peasant revolts, but those revolts were on a much smaller scale than the social upheavals in Europe, such as religious wars, the English or the French revolutions.

Koreans had a peculiar way of appointing the heir to the throne. Korean monarch (wang) usually selected an heir during his lifetime. Any male descendent of him could become wang's successor, not only his eldest son, and the monarch could change his mind any time and select a new successor. And he had quite a choice, since besides his wife (wang could only have one), a Korean monarch had a couple of dozen concubines, and any of his offspring by any woman could become his heir.

The unhurried pace of the life in ancient Korea is, I think, best understood when you look at labels in South Korean museum. A label next to some ancient blunderbuss or fusil states succinctly: "Weapon from the Joseon period," and that period lasted from 1392 when general Yi Seong-gye, subsequently known as king Taejo, founded the Yi dynasty, until 1910, when Japan annexed Korea. The Yi dynasty was preceded by the Goryeo dynasty which also had ruled the Korean Peninsula for over four hundred years.

Korea has always been strongly influenced by China. For fifteen hundred years, since the emergence of the first Korean states in the 3rd and 4th centuries up until the late 19th century, Old Chinese was Korea's official language used for business correspondence, for Korea's extensive chronicles, for publicizing laws. All the elite literature was produced in the Old Chinese as well. Hangul, Korea's national writing system, was derisively labeled "women's writing" meaning that only women and commoners used it, and educated men should use only the cultured language, that is, Old Chinese. Korean intellectuals and officials should have been fluent in Old Chinese and should also have mastered the classical Chinese cultural tradition.

Only in 1894-1896, Korean became the country's official language. Yet for many decades afterwards, fluency in Old Chinese was mandatory for any educated Korean, and until quite recently, Chinese characters were widely used in books written in Korean to render borrowed words.

Chinese influence in Korea wasn't limited to language and literature only. For many centuries, the Korean state had been modeled on the Chinese one. The number and functions of ministries, the rules for officialdom, state rituals in old Korea imitated Chinese models. In essence, the Korean government of the Yi dynasty (the Joseon period, 1392-1910) was a small-scale model of the Chinese government of the Tang and Song dynasties. They had similar names for the majority of the governmental bodies, they had similar functions, similar hierarchy, supervision principles, although the number of officials in Korea was much smaller.

The Gyenbokgung wooden palace complex built in Seoul in 1394, home to the Korean royal family for more than five hundred years, is strikingly similar to the Forbidden Palace in Beijing. There are similar architectural details, plaques indicating the seating order for officials during royal audiences, etc.

Wangs, Korea's kings, regularly sent various gifts to the Chinese Emperor, but it wasn't so much tribute as it was the acknowledgement of his supremacy as the Ruler of the Universe. That is why reciprocating gifts sent to Seoul from Beijing were oftentimes more precious than the Korean gifts. Wangs were obliged to give the Chinese emperor military aid in those campaigns China sometimes waged near Korean borders. In exchange, China offered Korea its protection, defended Korea from invasions and, most importantly, didn't invade Korea.

Communicating with Koreans: The First Experience

I first had to deal with a South Korean in the Union of Myanmar where I was posted as the Ambassador of the Russian Federation in 1997. The United Nations High Commissioner for Refugees (UNHCR) carried out a so-called rehabilitation program in Myanmar, to put it plainly, the UNHCR provided aid to the Rohingyas. These are Muslims, ethnic Bengalees living in Myanmar near the border with Bangladesh. For various reasons which have no bearing on my story, in the 1990s, a large number of the Rohingyas crossed the border into Bangladesh to that country's annoyance. Bangladesh filed a complaint with the UN, Myanmar was forced to take the Rohingyas back, and the UNHCR started the above-mentioned program. They set up camp in a remote place in the jungle and invited numerous experts from various counties from Sweden to Australia and from Guatemala to Malawi. The experts started to teach the Rohingyas to grow potatoes, trade in rice and beans, and dig irrigation ditches all of which they, being country people, could very well do all by themselves. That program, sanctified with the UN clout, was given a lot of money, yet the money was never enough, which was no surprise since everyone involved, besides getting some stupendous salaries, also availed themselves of frequent, all-expenses-paid vacations to any part of the world and of many other additional perks. Therefore an enterprising Italian in charge of the program periodically arranged jungle trips for ambassadors accredited to Yangon. The ambassadors had to see for themselves how effective his work was and to ask their respective governments to pour more money into the program.

When I went on my first and only jungle trip, it turned out, the Italian had gone over the top with invitations, and besides the ambassadors to Yangon, the UNHCR camp was also visited by ambassadors to Bangkok who were also accredited to Myanmar. Therefore, some ambassadors could not be given single rooms. We were put into doubles, and we drew lots to determine our roommates. My lot threw me in with the South Korean whom I had only briefly met upon arrival to Yangon, when paying protocol visits to my colleagues from the diplomatic corps.

Frankly, I was somewhat uneasy about the situation, and I also sensed my roommate shared my unease. We both were uncomfortable for the same reason: it was my first close encounter with a South Korean, and it was his first close encounter with a Russian. We were roommates for three days, and never before had I had such a considerate person to share accommodation with. I believe my South Korean colleague's impression of me was equally favorable. We became friends, and his wife later taught my wife to cook the pride and joy of the Korean cuisine, the Kimchee cabbage, and she approached it very seriously: we were sent a videotape with the cooking process, a book in English with the history of kimchee, and the ingredients required to obtain a fine end result. Thanks to my South Korean colleague, we became so enthralled with the kimchee culture that the first museum we went to in Seoul was the kimchee museum in the elegant modern COEX building. By the time we arrived in Seoul, my South Korean friend from Yangon had already retired from the Korean Ministry of Foreign Affairs, but he continued to work, he was a business consultant, and we met regularly.

Koreans are No-Nonsense People

As I have already mentioned, I studied Hindi at the university, and I am still fluent in it. Although virtually every educated Indian speaks English, the knowledge of Hindi helped me a lot in India where I spent a total of 11 years. And knowing language isn't important just to be able to live a comfortable everyday life, to shop easily, or to travel around the country. When you know the language, you understand the people's mindset better, you are able to see various things as if through their eyes. It is as if a door is opened for you into the inner world of the country. When I was appointed Ambassador to Myanmar, I spent a year studying Burmese; I learned to get around in the city, to read newspaper headlines, to make short protocol speeches.

However, things didn't go so well with Korean. Having learned about my appointment to Seoul, I went to Professor T.A. Novikova, Russia's top authority on Korean, asking to recommend a good teacher. Yet not only she didn't oblige, moreover, she advised against studying Korean. For a Russian, or for a speaker of any Indo-European language, Korean is very difficult, and it's not the matter of the writing system. Hangul is not like the Chinese characters, you can learn it in about a month. Pronunciation is also not a problem, many Korean sounds which are difficult, say, for the Japanese, are typical for the Russian language. It is the matter of the very system of the Korean language. It takes long and regular everyday studies to internalize it, and even a week-long break is enough to reduce the preceding efforts to nothing. Koreans, on the other hand, are perfectionists, and they will have no respect for an ambassador who speaks awkward Korean. So, Professor Novikova said, study literature on Korea in Russian and English, and leave speaking Korean to interpreters.

And I followed her advice, especially since the Embassy's two young interpreters were highly praised by Koreans. There was a difference between them, though.

One of them studied Korean in Seoul, and South Koreans used to say that should they close their eyes when he was speaking, they would believe he is a South Korean. The other one graduated from a university in North Korea, and although South Koreans acknowledged his excellent command of the language, they would sometimes joke that he sounded like the Pyongyang radio.

Many Russians and westerners alike complain that Koreans are difficult to deal with. I believe it depends on the expectations. Unlike Europeans, Koreans are less likely to engage in the so-called "small talk" about nothing in particular. They are very no-nonsense people and they wouldn't waste time on chatting "of cabbages and kings," although, truth be told, how many Russian politicians and businessmen excel at small talk?

Just like Russians, Koreans can be prompted into a lively conversation if the subject is of interest for them, if it touches upon their business or hobby, particularly golf, and if the conversation is generously lubricated with drinks.

Drinking for Koreans is a strict ritual dictating how to pour the liquor, what toasts to say, and how to respond to those toasts.

For instance, the guest of honor at a banquet will be served a drink called "the A-bomb." This bomb is in essence *yorsh* so well-known to Russian drunkards, a mixture of beer and something stronger, be it Korean *soju*, vodka, or whiskey. But the ritual itself! First a small shot glass of about 60 grams appears, then comes a large tumbler of the same design, holding about 300 grams. The strong drink is solemnly poured into the shot glass, then the shot glass is placed on the bottom of the tumbler which is then filled with beer. Then the drink is served to the person being toasted. The ceremony can be repeated several times, with obvious results. However, to avoid undesirable consequences, the guest of honor can delegate the duty to drink "the bomb" to someone from his group. Naturally, the partiers disband full of warmest regard for each other.

Koreans are mostly very musical and love singing. They have beautiful melodic songs. Europeans, though, have an ambivalent attitude to Korean folk music, because it has too much drum beat.

Any and every official negotiation and private conversation with Koreans, even those which touched upon some unpleasant subjects, were, in my experience, invariably conducted with consideration and respect.

I remember only one unpleasant episode. I was invited to dinner by a fairly prominent public figure. He got drunk rather quickly and began to discourse on rapid changes in our lives. There used to be the USSR, a super-power, and what do we have now in its stead? And the Russian-Korean border along the Tumangan is agreed upon with Pyongyang only, and Seoul's stance on that border after the country is reunited remains to be seen, etc. I got up, saying I had no desire to listen to such talk, and went home.

Koreans are very punctual. Being late for a meeting is almost an insult. If you say some event will start at 7 pm, rest assured that by 6:45 pm, most guests will have arrived. The same applies to the end of a reception. In Seoul, no one stays for a long time over coffee, as if often happens in Moscow. Everybody understands that both the host and the guests have things to do in the morning, and it's best to be well rested by then, especially since mornings in Seoul start early, and a business breakfast is just that at 7:30 am, and important political issues or large contracts are not discussed over steak and a glass of wine, but over a glass of orange juice with an omelet and porridge. I often attended such breakfasts and even gave talks to businessmen when everybody consumed their porridge and omelets first, and then listened to the guest speaker.

"Are You Perchance Hungry?"

Apropos of food. During their history, Koreans often experienced famine, and they developed a very respectful, careful, and even reverential attitude to food, similar to that of people who survived the Siege of Leningrad during World War II. You cannot leave food on your plate, you cannot throw food away. Sharing food, giving food to even a drop-by guest is the unbreakable rule in Korea. Korean protocol greeting, similar to the English "How are you?," literally means "Aren't you perchance hungry?"

Korean cuisine has a lot in common with the Chinese and the Japanese ones. Just like the Chinese and the Japanese, Koreans like pork and eat lots of it. Beef is rare and a lot more expensive. Just like the Japanese, Koreans eat a lot of seafood and fish, but they prefer sea fish, not fresh-water fish.

Korean cuisine is quite spicy, they particularly like the chili pepper. Korea, particularly in the south, has a warm, humid climate, and the pepper helps preserve food for longer. Korean dishes haven't always been spicy. Chili pepper made its way into Korea only as late as the 16th century when it was imported by Portuguese seafarers. This spice comes from America, yet it became such an inalienable part of the Korean cuisine that it became its distinguishing feature. It is the chili pepper that gives Korean dishes their distinctive red-orange color, and in modern Korean, the same word means both "spicy" and "tasty."

Garlic is yet another essential part of the Korean cuisine. Since eating garlic given by the divine Hwanung turned a she-bear into a beautiful woman and the mother of Dangun, the progenitor of all Koreans, they believe in garlic's near-magic powers, grow lots of it and eat it in large amounts even in the morning.

Just like in other Asian countries, Koreans eat a lot of rice. For Koreans, it's what bread is for people in Europe. Rice is served to everyone in an individual bowl, and other snacks are put on large plates to be shared.

Rice is usually served with a lot of vegetables, usually pickled and very spicy, and particularly with kimchee, Koreans' favorite dish. Just one mentioning of kimchee is enough to make a Korean smile a happy smile, like Ukrainians at the mentioning of fatback. If American photographers ask people to say "cheese," Koreans say "kimcheeeee" with the final "eee" pronounced as a very long one.

"Kimchee" may mean anything: cabbage, turnips, cucumbers, beans, ferns, seaweed, mushrooms, herring, shrimp, pork ears – anything that can be pickled with the spicy sauce made of chili pepper, black pepper, garlic, onions, ginger, seafood paste, and mugwort. Korean families usually have a special fridge for kimchee (the dish has a very pungent smell), and it is invariably served for every lunch and dinner.

In the west, Koreans are castigated for eating dogs. Koreans aren't the only ones to do it. People in Vietnam, South China, and Polynesia eat dogs far more often. However, Koreans are usually the ones to be subjected to angry criticism. The most popular Korean dog meat dish is the Boshintang soup which translates as "the soup of longevity." Traditionally in Korea, this dish is credited with many healing properties. People believe it prolongs life, promotes better health, and even makes men more virile. Boshintang is traditionally served in the hot Korean summer.

Historically, Koreans started eating dog meat not because they were particularly savage, but due to purely economic reasons. Land is a precious commodity on the Korean Peninsula, there is simply no space to graze cows or sheep, and a special breed of meat dog was the ancient Koreans' discovery which allowed them to add protein to their diet comprising mostly rice and kimchee.

No one in Korea eats pets or guard dogs. Special dogs are bred and fattened, just like pigs, with no one forming a particular attachment to them. Dog meat is not an everyday part of Koreans' diet.

Recent surveys showed than more than 50 per cent of Koreans have never tried dog meat. Only older people eat it, mostly men. They are willing to pay a lot of money to follow the tradition. In restaurants, Boshintang costs 35 dollars and up. An average tourist will have to expend a lot of effort to find a restaurant serving this delicacy. Restaurants are not allowed to include Boshintang and other dog meat dishes in their regular menus. They are served on customer request only.

Debates concerning eating dog meat have been going on for decades by now. In South Korea itself, people take various stances on the matter. There are many opponents of this tradition. They are mostly young people who grew up watching western movies and reading western books where the dog is man's best friend, and not a dish. Small, almost toy dogs, like Yorkshire terriers, are becoming increasingly popular among the young generation, and even among older Koreans. The owners lavish attention on their pets, dress them to current dog fashion and dye them various bright colors.

A traditional Korean table is laid with many bowls, plates, and cups. A strict order was started several centuries ago, and it is still observed, and in accordance with this order, food is divided into appetizers and main courses. The number of appetizers allows to see what kind of a meal that is: whether it celebrates the birth of a child, an anniversary, or whether it is just a family dinner. 12 appetizers mark the so-called Emperor's meal.

Traditionally, Koreans use chopsticks, but they also use spoons since Korean cuisine has a variety of soups. A spoon in the Korean culture is a symbol of life: if a family has four children, in Russia we would speak of four mouths, and Koreans speak about four spoons. When someone dies, people say that "he put his spoon down."

Korean cuisine is very healthy, it is very low on fat and sugar. For dessert, Koreans usually serve fruit and not sweets, and that goes even for official receptions, and fruit are not some exotic things like mango or rambutan, but traditional local apples, pears, persimmons, and strawberries which are particularly good in winter.

Healthy food ensures Koreans' long life; today, life expectancy is 77 years for men and almost 84 years for women. Healthy food also ensures fitness. There are very few obese people among those over forty. Obesity is evident among teenagers only, those who are victims of hamburgers and French fries served by McDonald's which is spreading its tentacles through Korean cities. Improved quality of life provides better nutrition: people now eat more fish and meat, and as a result, average life expectancy grew by 26 years, and the average height increased by 20 centimeters. One Korean film director complained that when he had been making a film about the Korean war he had had trouble finding both actors and extras; people were mostly too well-fed for the film to look realistic.

Koreans are quite addicted to their cuisine. Many of my friends complained that a few days abroad without kimchee made them miserable. Some Koreans take kimchee on their foreign business trips, there are special plastic containers on sale for that purpose. Korean tourists create difficulties abroad when they insist on eating in Korean restaurants only.

Koreans have a tradition of giving food sets as holiday gifts for friends and acquaintances. Before Chuseok, the Korean Thanksgiving in September, before Christmas and the lunar New Year, the windows of the most expensive supermarkets are adorned with beautifully gift-wrapped food sets including meats, dried fish, vegetables, and fruit. My wife and I also received such gifts. For instance, we may receive a box carefully wrapped in pink silk fabric with a card from a minister or even the prime minister himself saying: "Happy holiday!" We unwrap it and see carefully sliced meat or a string of dried fish. A very kind and touching tradition.

However, certain Korean customs take some getting used to. For instance, a Russian who has come to Korea for the first time will be rather unpleasantly struck by flower wreaths with ribbons, often surrounding entrances into shops or offices. For us, such wreaths look as if they belong at a funeral. However, in Korea such wreaths are our equivalent of a basket of flowers, and the ribbons proclaim happy wishes and congratulations, and not condolences. Sometimes, when attending some function or other, such as a reception at the Embassy, I would see entire galleries of wreaths sent by friends and firms doing business with Russia.

Know Your Place!

"Know your place" is the social law in the Korean society which clearly retains its peasant roots and is in essence a family, just like the Russian peasant commune used to be. A German or a Frenchman wouldn't address a stranger in the street as "my old man," as a Russian would do, and neither would they address a woman they don't know as "Ajumoni," "auntie," as a Korean would. A German or French society with its long-standing city bourgeois traditions is in essence a market with its neutral, formally polite forms of address such as "Herr," "monsieur," "Frau," "madam," etc. which don't have this exceedingly familiar, but extremely kind-hearted ring as "my old man" or "Ajumoni."

Just like children in an old-time Russian peasant family, every Korean child learns to behave the right way, that is, to obey his or her elders, "to be seen, not heard," in other words, to be "like everybody else." Only then a Korean will be part of "woori," a certain community, be it family, a group of colleagues at work, the entire Korean nation. A Korean without a woori, be it a student club, a trade union, or an air force vets' club, is completely and utterly lost. He or she is virtually defenseless. Vladimir Mayakovsky, a great Soviet poet, might have been writing just about such a Korean when he wrote, "A man alone is nonsense, a zero." Woori protects Koreans from a hostile environment, it helps them bounce back should they hit a rough patch, it supports them in their work and career.

Yet there is another distinctive feature of the peasant family along with mutual help and support, and that is its strict hierarchy. Korean family has strict rules: the father merits greater respect than the mother, brothers are more respected than sisters, the wife obeys her husband, after her husband's death, the mother obeys her eldest son.

The same applies to the Korean society as a whole. In accordance with Confucian ethics, a Korean's social world is vertical and divided into precise structures: older – younger, superior - subordinate. A Korean man or a Korean woman might call their friend or colleague "brother" or "sister," but it will inevitably be "older brother" or "younger sister." When Koreans are in a hurry to exchange business cards with the person they meet for the first time, they don't do it because they are particularly polite or want to learn and remember the name of their new acquaintance. They want to be sure what place this person holds in the societal hierarchy, determine that person's rung on the social ladder, and form relations with him or her accordingly. Seniority is usually determined by office or position held, but also by age. A western woman shouldn't be shocked when a Korean woman enquires about her age right away. For a Korean woman, it's not some trick question or a tactless inquiry; this is a purely practical issue, the Korean woman has to determine her future manner in relation to the new acquaintance depending on whether she is younger or older.

The patriarchal nature of the Korean society is also evident in the relations between employees in private businesses and in governmental bodies. Even the lowest-ranking supervisor in a firm has absolute authority for his or her subordinates, just like a peasant paterfamilias. Their requests are obeyed without a murmur of complaint, and their reproaches and criticisms cause an acute feeling of guilt and a burning desire to correct the mistake immediately. At the same time, every Thursday, the entire staff of a department or an organization, regardless of their attitude to alcohol, proceed to have a drinking session, sometimes with drinks flowing very freely, they go bar-hopping until hopping turns into bar-crawling. During such outings, any employee can, in a respectful manner, share their private problems with the boss, and the boss will listen to them like a father, and, should the situation permit, will show understanding. Why Thursdays, why not Fridays, right before the weekends? The reason is simple: having got drunk on Thursday night, people will suffer through the hangover on Friday at work, and they will devote Saturday and Sunday to their family, and for family time, you must be cheerful and kind, while " the day after the night before"hangover would make it impossible.

Foreign visitors often remark on how prudish South Korea is compared to Europe, the US, Australia, and even Japan. Of course, Koreans aren't saints. Men, including men with wives and children, happen to get drunk and visit "working girls" of whom there are many in the Korean cities, even though prostitution is illegal. Yet South Korea has no drug problem, South Koreans virtually don't know what homosexuality is, and they disapprove of what we call "common-law marriage." In Korea, getting married and starting a family is an obligatory and inevitable stage in a person's life, a duty to one's parents and family. If a man is unmarried at 28-30, or a woman at 25, their parents, relatives, friends, or even bosses will always start looking for a spouse for them. That's why it is virtually impossible in Korea to meet an unmarried man over 35 or an unmarried woman over 30.

Korean family is one of the factors that made the "Korean economic miracle" possible. Marriage in Korea is concluded once and forever. And even though marriages in Korea are still often arranged by the parents of the groom and bride, or with the help of matchmakers, outwardly they seem quite stable. By European or Russian standards, divorce is relatively rare. The public opinion about divorces is extremely negative. A divorced couple doom themselves to disapproving stares and also to some serious trouble. A new marriage is difficult for a divorced man and next to impossible for a divorced woman. A divorce may often ruin the career of a state official, a politician, and, however strange it may seem to a European or an American, of a celebrity.

In Korea, abandoned children and single mothers are impossible. Even if the parents live separately, they are still a family as far as people around them are concerned, and together they take part in all the traditional family celebrations. In Korea, children live with their parents at least until they get married themselves, and one of the children, usually the eldest son, continues to live with his parents even after getting married. He should take care of the parents and make their old age free of care and financial worries.

What do these customs have to do with economic growth? They have direct bearing on the economy. Comparing Korea to western states of similar level of economic development, we will see that Korea bears a significantly smaller burden of various social payments such as pensions, stipends, and welfare subsidies. In western countries, the divorce rate is very high, which leads to a high number of single mothers and large sums in support payments to them. In the West, children traditionally leave home and don't support their parents, and consequently, the governments expend sizable amounts on pensions and maintaining retirement homes (in the US, going into a retirement home is a standard situation!). Since in the West, children usually leave home at the age of 18-19 and no longer count on their parents' support, the state has to come up with various financial plans to allow them to receive an education.

In Korea, there is no need for that. Korea has to maintain a huge (in proportion to its population) army and powerful secret services. A strong Korean family relieves the state of many concerns allowing it to concentrate on the most important things such as defense, foreign relations development, building the economic infrastructure.

Korean Wife is a Homemaker

Naturally, Koreans, just like any other nation, have their family issues. The most pressing one is women's subservient situation which is a holdover since the Middle Ages when the Korean society in its everyday life was guided by the "respect men, despise women" principle.

Just a few decades ago, South Korean family and inheritance law openly discriminated against women. Only in 1991, they introduced legal changes which allowed women to be head of the household, acknowledged their rights to a share in the family's property, and gave women more rights to see children after divorce.

In the morning, Seoul fills up with people hurrying to work, and many are young girls and women wearing fashionable western-style clothes (I think Korean women generally pay more attention to their appearance than, say, the Japanese women), but there are hardly any women over thirty, not to mention middle-aged ones. That's because most women quit work after they get married. Traditionally in Korea, women had no place in either business or public life. Ideally, a Korean wife is a homemaker. She should keep a comfortable home for her husband and bring up the children. It applies to all social strata, but first and foremost, it applies to the middle class, i.e. families with decent income and nowadays, with both spouses having a higher education. Korean women mostly accept the situation, especially since in the vast majority of Korean families, it is the women who hold the purse strings.

This situation is also reflected in the South Korean social life. Many events which in Europe or the US you normally attend with your wife, in Seoul or Busan are attended by men exclusively. Korean men come up with bizarre excuses to attend even Embassy receptions or official dinners without their spouses. It is also worth noting that when a Korean man does attend a reception with his wife, he is far from happy when some foreigner he does not know starts paying his wife even the most innocent of compliments. For Koreans, complimenting another man's wife is kind of tactless. In general, women should keep their own company, and Korean women adhere to this principle, keeping their own company and keeping their husbands out of it. There are lots of clubs for women dedicated to a huge variety of subjects; women happily study the art of Ikebana, batik, or make jewelry. In separate rooms in prestigious restaurants you can often observe large companies of women well over forty, well-groomed, with impeccably done hair, dressed fashionably, and having loud conversation and bursting out laughing over a glass of wine or ever something stronger.

Even if our feminists come down hard on me for saying that, society undoubtedly benefits from the fact that South Korea is a country of housewives. And the main benefit is that children are always well-supervised. Little kids are always fed on time and dressed in clean clothes; in the morning, mothers take them to kindergartens, and when they start school, mothers take turns keeping watch before and after lessons at their children's schools, making sure passing drivers slow down. There are no teenagers loitering about in South Korean cities, with nothing to occupy themselves with. Mothers make sure that, besides schoolwork, their children attend some extra classes, do sports or study music.

To women should go things that are women's, and to men then things that are men's. But a growing number of South Korean women want to go beyond their home, however prosperous and equipped with the latest gadgets it might be, beyond their sophisticated sitting rooms, and women's clubs; they want to do something else in life besides caring for their husband and children; after all, they didn't receive higher education for nothing. South Korean women become more and more active in politics: in 1990, out of 299 members of the National Assembly, the South Korean parliament, only 6 were women, in 2010, they were 44 women. Women gradually establish themselves in business, too. At the same time, the way to the top both in politics and in business is open first and foremost for those women who have or used to have a strong man's support.

For instance, here are four most famous South Korean women of today included into Forbes 100 Most Influential Women. Two are politicians, and two are businesswomen. Only one of them, Han Myung Sook, the first and so far only woman to have held the office of South Korea's Prime Minister in 2006-2007, came to power on her own merits alone. She is an eminent academic and educator, she gained prominence participating in the democratic movements during military dictatorships, she fought for women's rights. In 1979-1981, she was imprisoned. After 2000, she was twice elected to the National Assembly. Before becoming Prime Minister, she was the Minister for Women's Affairs and for the Environment.

Another major woman politician is the country's current president Park Geun-hye. She was elected to Parliament four times; she had been the leader of the ruling party, she has an impressive charisma and leadership qualities. But she undoubtedly owes her victory in the 2012 presidential elections to the fact that she is the daughter of president Park Chung-hee who paved the way for the "Korean economic miracle."

Now let's take a look at the world of business. Lee Myung-hee is the richest woman in the country, the eighth in the list of South Korean billionaires with a personal fortune of 1.5 billion dollars. She is the chairperson of the quickly growing Shinsegae retail chain which includes the world's largest department store in the South Korean city of Busan, the store which in 2009 surpassed even New York's famous Macy's department store. Lee Myung-hee would have been unlikely to be such a success hadn't she been the daughter of Lee Byung-chull, the founder of Samsung, and the younger sister of Lee Kun-hee, Samsung's current chairman. Hyun Jeong-eun, current chairperson of Hyundai Group, took the reins in 2003, after the death of the previous chairman Chung Mong-hun, her husband.

This list can go on. And the business dynasties of the two businesswomen I mentioned are continued. Lee Myung-hee's daughter Chung Yoo-kyung recently became vice president of Shinsegae.

Imported Brides

Overwhelming changes are taking over every aspect of life in South Korea, including marriages and family. Korea is a monoethnic country, and marriages with people from other ethnicities are almost inevitably marriages with foreigners, nationals of other countries. Between the 15th and the late 20th centuries, Korea maintained nearly total isolation from the outside world, and interethnic marriages were extremely rare. Even as late as twenty years ago, South Korea knew virtually no mixed marriages and marriages with foreigners. Of all East Asian countries, Korea viewed mixed marriages in the most negative light. There were instances of Korean women marrying foreigners, mostly American soldiers stationed in Korea, and going abroad to live in their husband's countries, yet such cases were infrequent, too.

Now the situation is different. Marriages with foreigners are now quite wide-spread in Korea. Statistics tell us that over the last 5-7 years, about 10 per cent of all marriages in Korea have been marriages to foreign nationals. In 2011 (the most recent year with fully published statistics), marriages to foreigners made up 9 per cent of all registered marriages in Korea. A closer look reveals that three quarters of them are marriages between South Korean men and women from other countries, mostly from China and Vietnam. For instance, in 2011, there were 29,700 marriages to foreigners in Korea, and half of them were marriages between Korean men and Vietnamese and Chinese women.

Imported brides are a widespread phenomenon now. There is a large number of marriage agencies in Korea, which find foreign brides for South Korean men. The Internet is full of advertisements of this nature, complete with photographs.

The reason for this development lies first and foremost in the changes that affected South Korean village life. A typical marriage between a Korean and a foreigner is a marriage between a Korean peasant (of middle age between 35-45, and of no particular success in his village) and a young girl, ten t0 twenty years his junior, from Vietnam or China. It is not accidental that the number of marriages to foreigners is particularly high in agricultural regions where the disproportion between sexes is particularly obvious.

In recent decades, Korean girls leave villages for cities far more often than young men. Girls prefer to work set hours in an air-conditioned factory, rather than toil in a rice or potato field from morning till night, rain or shine. They yearn for the entertainments the city offers, they want to have free hand in spending the money they make. There are lots of things they want. We know it from our own experience in Russia. And young men stay in villages with their parents, preserving family traditions on the plot of land they inherited from their ancestors, and they need wives for their family to live on.

Even ethnic Korean women from China, Uzbekistan, Kazakhstan, Kyrgyzstan, and particularly Vietnamese and Filipino women have hard time adjusting to life in South Korean families. Their mothers-in-law and older in-laws in general are rarely pleased to welcome a foreigner into their family. Mixed-marriage children are called Kosian, not Korean, and are often treated in schools as if they didn't belong there. The word Kosian is considered a slur by those who would want to see themselves as Korean, and the Korean Amnesty International considers it a manifestation of racial discrimination.

South Korean authorities work actively toward helping "imported wives" adjust to living in South Korea. Korean language courses, classes on national customs are meant to make the transition smoother. At the same time, one should not discard the possibility that the appearance of many foreign wives will noticeably change the Korean society.

Hanbok, Hanok, and Ondol

Today, Koreans dress mostly according to the Western fashion. Office dress code is clearly conservative. In governmental offices and in private companies both men and women must wear classical suits in dark colors.

No bright ties or scarves, no tweed jackets - those are for university professors only, and no pants for girls, they must wear skirts only, and those skirts for both young girls and older women, in offices and in any public space, should meet certain requirements. From March 22, 2013, South Korean authorities re-introduced the prohibition to wear "indecent clothes" which had been repealed in 2006. The list of indecent clothes includes, among other items, mini-skirts. Those who breach this prohibition and "provoke embarrassment and discomfort in people around them" with their appearance can be fined 50 thousand won (about $45).

The Korea Times wrote that South Korean public was

vehemently opposed to this law since, as many people believed, it pushed the country back into the 1970s, when Park Chung-hee, the father of the current president, was the head of state. At that time, South Korea also had a strict dress code: police stopped and fined girls wearing mini-skirts, gave forcible haircuts to men with long hair, and busted underground clubs playing rock music.

Koreans try not to "provoke embarrassment and discomfort in people around them" by their casual dress as well. In the streets of Seoul and other cities, there are no men wearing shorts and short-sleeved shirts. Korean women go swimming on public beaches wearing dresses, not bikinis. However, they are "covered up" not because they don't want people to ogle them, but because they are afraid to get suntanned. Koreans are obsessed with light skin since historically, only peasants working their fields in the sun were swarthy, while the nobility spent their time lounging in palace chambers and therefore had light skin. Women in South Korea stock up on anything and everything that lightens the skin. Leading cosmetics companies produce special creams and cosmetics with skin-lightening effect for the Korean market.

Even though Koreans are "westerners" in their everyday dress, on solemn occasions, they wear their national clothes. For family reunions, for holidays such as a baby's first birthday, a wedding, a New Year celebration, a 60th or a 70th birthday which are of special significance for Koreans, they wear colorful national clothes, the so-called hanbok.

Hanbok is made from bright one-color fabrics. Traditional women's hanbok consists of chogori, a blouse shirt or a jacket, and chima, a full wrap-around skirt. Men's hanbok consists of chogori and paji, baggy pants. Baggy paji are designed for sitting on the floor. Paji are a one-size-fits-all garment since they are fastened with two strings in the front.

Koreans are still fond of their traditional house, hanok. There used to be two types of hanok, with a tiled roof for the nobility, and with a thatched roof for peasants and commoners. Now the thatched hanok is all but gone, but the tiled hanok can be seen in the country and even in the cities. Supporting framework is made out of wood, with bricks of compressed earth mixed with grass used for the infill; in living quarters, the floor is wooden, and in utility rooms, it is either stone or earthen.

A distinguishing feature of a traditional Korean house is ondol, its heating system. In Chinese, "ondol" means "warm cavities." The system is believed to have been invented 2,000 years ago. This is how it works. A stove is located in the kitchen, or built into an outer wall of a room. Under the room's floor, there are horizontal cavities (tunnels) to allow smoke and hot air pass when the stove is stoked with wood. Ondol was designed in such a way as to retain heat for a long time.

Heating floors using the ondol heating system is traditional for Korean houses. This heating system obviates the need for beds and chairs, since Koreans preferred to sleep and seat on the warm floor, using only thin mats or mattresses. This life "on the floor" had a huge impact on Koreans' everyday life, and this life is still largely retained. Today, many Koreans live in European-type houses or in multi-storey apartment buildings where the place of ondol has been taken by an improved system of water floor heating. That also explains why Koreans don't manufacture woolen or silk carpets which are so widespread in other parts of Asia. People walk barefoot at home, that's why you must take off your street shoes when entering a Korean apartment.

And most Koreans, including the affluent and European-educated ones, still sleep on the floor. An eminent South Korean industrialist once invited several ambassadors, including me and my wife, to a housewarming party in his newly-built country house near Seoul. The house was equipped with the most sophisticated gadgets to make it comfortable. The guests were shown a bedroom decorated in the current European fashion with a magnificent king-size bed. The bedroom, however, looked unlived in. The host said that he and his wife didn't sleep in that fashionable western bedroom, preferring instead a traditional Korean bedroom without beds.

Beauty at Any Cost.

Fans of South Korean TV shows and pop music know that most Korean celebrities are impeccably beautiful, with an ideal nose, huge almond-shaped eyed, and white skin without a single blemish. Korean idols are an example for the Korean youth and for the entire Asia. Statistics say that South Korea is the world leader in plastic surgery. In Seoul, one woman in five has had some type of plastic surgery, and many men have it done, too. Korea is filled with "before" and "after" ads for various plastic surgery clinics. Many parents pay for their children's surgery as their coming-of-age gift, or as a reward for good grades in school.

The Korean ideal is a narrow face with huge, anime-like, or, as Koreans call them, European eyes. Korean plastic surgeons work miracles. Although they say that those young people who come to their clinics today sometimes are more familiar with the recent trends in plastic surgery, and about what and how should be done. Their parents fully support them because in Korea, people believe that all the doors are open for beautiful people. And vacation time means a lot of work for plastic surgeons. Going to have a plastic surgery is like going to your dentist.

Blepharoplasty, eye surgery, is the most popular procedure (it is called *singapori*). It costs about $ 800, and however odd it may sound, it's a very popular gift given by parents to their children when they are about 20 on average. Blepharoplasty is followed by rhinoplasty (nose jobs), orthognathic surgery (facial bone manipulation), and lip enhancement.

The procedure for leg lengthening is gaining popularity. It can make legs up to 13 centimeters longer. Initially, the procedure was developed to help people with congenital defects or suffering the consequences of accidents. However, in South Korea today, the procedure is performed on anybody who is prepared to pay tens of thousands of dollars. This is how it works: telescoping rods are inserted into the sawed-apart femur, tibia, and fibula. Then the surgeon pulls the bones apart millimeter by millimeter, inducing the body to produce the graft (immature cells) which will eventually form the new bone material.

Not only are these procedures painful, they are also sometimes lethal. Yet Koreans continue to eagerly and enthusiastically "remodel" their bodies, aspiring to their dream. Kim Yu-mi, Miss Korea 2012, won the national competition and showed the entire country her lovely face and ideal body. Only later, school photos of Yu-mi were found on the Web, and on those photos, Miss Korea looks, to put it mildly, an entirely different person.

Red Crosses in Seoul's Night

Driving at night along Seoul's or Busan's many overpasses gives you a strange feeling. Everywhere, above and below, you see red neon crosses of Christian churches. South Korea in unique in that it is one of the few Asian states where Christianity, and particularly Protestantism, is an important component of today's culture.

Official statistics state that about 25 million South Koreans, that is, about half of the country's population, are believers. Out of them, 10.7 million are Buddhists, and nearly 14 million are Christians including 8.6 million Protestants and 5.2 million Catholics. South Korean Protestants are mostly Presbyterians and

Methodists. Syng Man Rhee, the first president of the Republic of Korea, was a Methodist. Lee Myong-bak, president in 2008-2013, and Kim Young-sam, president in 1993-1998, are Presbyterians. Liberal presidents Kim Dae-Jung and Roh Moo-Hyun who were in office between 1998 and 2008, were Catholics. Park Geun-hye, current president, is an atheist.

Interestingly, Protestantism and Catholicism in today's Korean statistics are treated as two different religions. When a Korean speaking Russian or English calls himself a Christian, it almost inevitably means he is a Protestant and not a Catholic or an Orthodox Christian.

Presbyterianism and Methodism made their way into Korea in 1884-1885 from the US, and this fact should be kept in mind when analyzing the situation in South Korea. How did American missionaries manage to settle in Korea so easily and painlessly? Competing Catholic missionaries and their Korean flock often had to give their lives for their faith. The most recent wave of persecutions against Catholics in Korea occurred in 1866, shortly before the arrival of Americans. A group of French missionaries were executed then. However, by the time Americans arrived, the Korean monarchy and statehood were severely weakened by the Japanese. Korea and Japan, locked in a political fight over the Korean Peninsula, couldn't care less about Christians. So American Presbyterian and Methodist missionaries managed to arrive at the favorable time of a power vacuum on the Korean Peninsula.

Although in the early 20th century, Christians made up only a small part of the population (1.5 per cent in 1911), they played a special part in those changes that had been taking place in Korea then. After Korea was annexed by Japan in 1910, the Protestant church was in essence fighting against the Japanese colonizers. At that time, Koreans didn't view Americans as colonizers, and whether Americans wanted to or not, they weren't able to plunder

Korea since the Japanese were hard at it. Missionaries took part in the social movements, in reforming the Korean way of thinking. Missionaries contributed to building schools, hospitals, universities, they introduced modern learning into the Korean society. A significant part was played by the financial support provided by America's rich religious communities.

In 1920s and 1930s, Christianity put down strong roots in Korea. Out of an alien faith introduced from the West, it turned into Korea's national religion. This is the key difference between the history of Christianity in Korea on the one hand and in the majority of Asian countries on the other. It is also largely tied to the fact that in Korea, the role of colonizers was assumed by the Japanese and not by Europeans who, at that time, were fond of emphasizing their Christian faith. Therefore, in Korea, persecuted Christian missionaries were perceived as the colonizers' enemies, and not as ideological agents of an alien power structure. Foreign missionaries' multifaceted educational activities contributed to the emergence of a new mindset, a new way of thinking. Korean youth learned about the code of bourgeois democratic freedoms, about such things as "constitution" and "parliament."

Consequently, over the span of the sixty years of Protestant missionary work, since 1885 until Korea's independence in 1945, Protestantism assumed leading positions in the country's spiritual life. Finally, during the colonial period, churches were places where people spoke their national language, church brochures were published in colloquial Korean, and they used Hangul, the national writing system. The new Korean intellectual elite, including nearly all leaders of the anti-colonial movement, were educated in Christian educational institutions. North Korea's leader Kim Il-sung came from a family of Protestant activists.

With the end of the Japanese colonial regime in 1945, some radical changes occurred. Christianity had no more barriers, prohibitions, and obstacles impeding its spread and development. Moreover, Christianity began to look more and more like an official ideology, it was supported by the state and received favorable treatment. Many political emigrants returned to Korea from the US, they were fervent Christians and preachers, and many of them assumed key offices in the state and key positions in society. After the Korean War, Christians in South Korea rapidly grew in numbers. In 1940, only 2.2 per cent of the population were Christians, in 1962, they were 12.8 per cent, and in 1990, 23 per cent.

Under the Syng Man Rhee's regime and during the subsequent military dictatorships (1948-1987), Christian clerics, communities and authorities were locked in complex and contradictory relations. On the one hand, the majority of Korean clerics supported the governmental ideology of intransigent anti-communism. The entire official western Christian world had by then assumed the anti-communist stance. Solid ties between Christian communities in South Korea and in the US also influenced the political attitudes of Korea's Protestant churches. It should be kept in mind that after 1945, the number of Christians among Korea's economic and political elite was very high, and it continued to increase, and that also made Christian churches rally for the preservation of the *status quo*. On the other hand, Korean Christianity never became a tool of the secular authorities. Korean Christians, particularly Korean Catholics, were active in various opposition movements. Catholic churches in Korea enjoy the unofficial, but generally recognized sanctuary right, and they often serve as venues for anti-government rallies. Catholic priests took part in anti-government rallies, they openly criticized the state's policies, they protected those who were persecuted by the authorities. Their actions reflected favorably on the image of the Christian church among the entire population, particularly among the intellectuals and students.

There is little doubt that the peculiar amalgamation of traditional Confucian values and Protestant beliefs in personal responsibility became a sort of a spiritual buttress in the South Korean modernization whereby it shed its backward feudal cast and became a postindustrial country. On the other hand, this amalgamation predetermined its spiritual ties to the US whence Presbyterian and Methodist missionaries arrived in Korea in the late 19th century.

In the 21st century, Christianity in Korea, unlike in the western countries, is on the rise, the number of Christians constantly increases, and the Christian ideology spans all the aspects of Korea's social life.

Korea's Pride

For a Korean working in a large corporation, such as Samsung, Hyundai, LG, SK, Doosan, his company is his protector and defender, his state which gives him wages, accommodation, health insurance. Sometimes, this state also pays for its employee's children to receive an education in engineering universities for them subsequently to join the ranks of its workers. No wonder the dance in such companies is led not merely by corporate patriotism, but by downright corporate chauvinism. In Samsung, for instance, every Monday starts with watching corporate cable news reporting on the new corporate achievements. The procedure concludes with the Samsung anthem to which employees should listen to with a proudly raised head.

Yet for a Korean, his company is also his family. Supervisors go to the same canteen as the rank-and-file employees, and they stand in the same line, because everyone who works in the company is a member of the same family. The bosses treat their subordinates with fatherly benevolence. If they want business to go well, people should be supported in their enthusiasm for their work. The best employees are held in high esteem and they are rewarded with bonuses and various signs of recognition.

At the wharves of Hyundai, Samsung, and Daewoo, I often took part in the launch ceremonies for tankers and other vessels built for Russian ship lines. And each time after Korean hosts, heads of shipbuilding companies, and Russian guests accepting the ships delivered their speeches, the floor was given to a large group of engineers, foremen, and average working stiffs: mechanics, maintenance personnel, metal workers, electricians, those very people who had built those gigantic ships with their own hands. The sea wind flapped the company's flags. Mini-fireworks exploded happily. A brass band in full-dress uniform and in white gloves enthusiastically played something extremely inspirational; very often it would be "Congratulations and Celebrations" by Cliff Richard, a British 1960s pop star. The names of the best workers were solemnly announced, they were given special commendation gifts, they were photographed together with the guests of honor. You had to be there to see the pride on those people's faces, they were proud of their work and of their company.

It is because people are proud of their company and of their country, that all the employees of Hyundai Motors, from the lowest ranker to the CEOs, will never be seen driving any other car but Hyundai. The President of the Republic of Korea and South Korean ambassadors to other countries use only Hyundai Equus cars. And although the name itself isn't quite Korean (*equus* is Latin for "horse") and the car itself is based on one of the Mitsubishi luxury car models, it is a car made in Korea, by Koreans, and for Koreans (and not only for them), it is no worse than luxury Mercedes or BMW. People in the Soviet Union used to be proud of the ZIS110 car used by Joseph Stalin and other Soviet leaders, although ZIS-110 bore a noticeable resemblance to Packard. Naturally, South Korean leaders also sport South

Korean equivalents of iPhones, iPads, and other gadgets made by Samsung or LG.

Westerners, and particularly Americans, being hard-core individualists, are critical of the Korean collectivism and the conformism that, unfortunately, often stems from this collectivism. They claim that the Confucian mindset impedes creative potential, turns a person into a mere follower of the will of his boss or master. There might be some truth to that, too. Any trailblazers, before making their discoveries, should doubt the traditional opinions held in their particular field, and the Confucian ethics certainly doesn't welcome such doubts. But what is best for society: when individuals diligently performs their duties while carefully observing the rules and norms, or the boundless energy of enterprising slap-dash workers ready to crush everything and anything in their creative quest? We saw a lot of the latter kind in Russia. A masterful surgery done by a brilliant surgeon will be pointless if next day, a slap-dash nurse will inject the patient with the wrong medicine, and even a perfect plane will crash if flown on low-quality fuel.

Since their childhood, Koreans are instilled with the conviction that any work should be done the right way, and if you do a poor job and will be, God forbid, found out, it will be a great shame. So they don't invent a bicycle and they don't live on the principle "it might be lousy, but we invented it ourselves." If a company realizes it cannot invent something innovative enough to startle the world, or if it, frankly speaking, fails no matter how hard it tries, it buys or "borrows" cutting-edge foreign technologies. And where they don't have Korean professionals, they invite the most knowledgeable foreign advisors: architects, engineers, scientists whose knowledge, skill, and competence they diligently adopt.

South Korean universities, cultural centers, and stadiums are remarkable. South Korea has a cult of education. Nine-year school education is mandatory: three years in elementary school and six years in intermediary school. The Republic of Korea is the third in the world in the number of college students; about fifty percent of schoolchildren go on to college. In 2009, Korea had 407 higher education institutions with 3.59 million students and 75.5 thousand faculty.

Most Korean universities are private. However, in Korea, unlike in the US, state universities are far more prestigious than the private ones, and the majority of talented and ambitious applicants want to be enrolled in a state, rather than a private university. The acronym SKY (with its reference to the English word "sky") stands for Korea's three most prestigious universities: S is for Seoul National University, a state institution, K is for Korean University (a private one), and Y is for Yonsei University, also a private university whose history starts with American missionaries of the late 19th - early 20th centuries. All three universities are in Seoul.

The top five of South Korean universities is rounded off with Korea Advanced Institute of Science and Technology, KAIST, a state institution founded in 1971 in Daejeon, and Pohang University of Science and Technology, a private institution founded in Pohand in mid-1980s. They are both among the world's top thirty engineering universities. People have reasons to believe that South Korea owes its breakthrough in hi-tech to the high quality education in those universities. It is noteworthy that in their concern for the country's future, South Korean authorities didn't fear being criticized by other countries for limiting their citizens' freedom of movement and they did forbid KAIST graduates to leave Korea to work abroad for five years after graduation. This is the South Korean way of preventing brain drain.

Each South Korean town has large, spacious centers with state-of-the-art equipment to serve as venues for world-famous performers, and in large cities with population over a million, for instance, in Busan, Incheon, Daegu, Daejeon, such centers are built in every city district, including residential neighborhoods. Sejeon Center of Seoul with its many halls and Seoul Arts Center are particularly impressive. Seoul Arts Center combines an opera house, a concert hall, a large exhibition hall, and many arts studios.

Due to extensive state support and to art patrons' generosity in the recent decades, western classical music became very popular in Korea, and there appeared a whole crop of world-class musicians, opera singers, and ballet dancers. However, the Koreans' principal cultural achievement is the so-called "Korean wave," the spread of Korean mass culture into other countries, first into the countries of Southeast Asia. China was the first to be hit by this wave, and the term "Korean wave" (*Hallyu*) itself was invented in China in 1990s. It started with "Sarani muogille" ("What love is"), a TV series which became a smash hit, and many more series and songs rode its coattails to success with the Chinese audience. Currently, the Korean Wave has covered over 60 countries, mostly in Southeast Asia: Taiwan, Japan, Thailand, the Philippines, etc. Korean culture is gradually spreading further and is gaining popularity in the Middle East and even in some African countries. Initially, pop music led the way, but now the songs are joined by cinema, cuisine, Taekwondo, etc.

The greatest success story is that of the pop singer Park Jae-sang whose stage name is Psy, derived from the English word "psycho." He is not particularly young (over thirty five), unlike Korean movie characters, he's not a sex symbol: below average height, slightly overweight, in funny round glasses, but today, he is the most popular Korean in the world, his popularity far exceeds even that of Ban Ki-moon, the UN Secretary General, and the latter is said to be mightily displeased with this fact. Psy's secret weapon is his "Gangnam Style" video. "Gangnam Style" is a Korean colloquialism referring to the posh way of life which Gangnam, a rich and fashionable Seoul district, is famous for. A rhythmical, quick-moving song accompanied by startling dancing moves is about "an ideal girl who knows when to be sophisticated and when to be wild." In 2012, the dance moves from this video were shown in news programs around the world, and afterwards, the video became the most-watched one in the entire history of YouTube. By December 21, 2012, it had been seen by more than a billion people: a first in the history of YouTube and the Internet. Psy's success is unique, too, because "Gangnam Style" became a hit in the US even though it is performed in Korean. It is the top seller in the iTunes stores in 31 countries.

In a way, Russia has also been hit by the Korean wave. Psy is parodied on Russian TV. Virtually every DVD store offers Korean movies dubbed into Russian. Some of them, especially those directed by Kim Ki-duk, are definitely worth watching. When it comes to Korean TV shows, their period dramas about various court intrigues are difficult to follow for the Russian audience since you need to know a lot of details about Korean life and history, and their soap operas are either too saccharine, or just shameless tear-jerkers.

South Korea is determined to excel at sports as well. At the 2004 Athens Olympics, South Korea came in 9th with 9 gold medals, 12 silver medals, and nine bronze medals, at the 2008 Beijing Olympics, South Korea came in 7th with thirteen gold medals, 10 silver medals, and eight bronze medals, and at the 2012 London Olympics, it came in 5th with thirteen gold medals, eight silver medals, and seven bronze medals. South Korea was also 5th at the 2010 Winter Olympics in Vancouver with five gold medals, six silver medals, and two bronze medals.

South Koreans excel at baseball, golf, archery, skeet shooting, table tennis, short track speed skating, figure skating, swimming, and, naturally, Taekwondo, a Korean martial art. Through South Korea's efforts, Taekwondo was included into Olympic sports and gained popularity throughout the world. Today, about 3,000 South Korean Taekwondo instructors work with athletes in over 150 countries across the globe.

An export-oriented country should have everything at the world-class level: manufacturing, hotels, roads, and, pardon the mundane turn, public restrooms. The situation with the latter conveniences is said to have been quite dire. Yet before the 1988 Seoul Olympics, the country's leaders (Roh Tae-woo was then president, and he was a tough retired general) tackled this question head-on, not "to lose face" before the foreign guests. Since then, both in Seoul and in other cities, the situation with public restrooms is fine. You can find free-of-charge and clean public restrooms everywhere: in subway stations, in underpasses, and in other places with large human traffic.

There Are No Protection Rackets in South Korea

South Korea knows virtually no street crime such as petty theft, hooliganism, street fraud. You can be a slack-jawed gawker walking around all day with a fat wallet sticking from your pants' pocket, and no one will attempt to steal it. If, on your way home, you leave your bag with an expensive purchase from some upscale boutique in some tiny shop, and having realized two hours later what happened, you will finally make your way to that shop, they will gladly reunite you with your bag which will be none the worse for wear. The streets are safe and interesting to walk at midnight and after midnight; in some Seoul neighborhoods, there are special nighttime markets which offer a wealth of goods. Owners of little shops often leave their goods in the street unattended. I remember my first week in Seoul, when I was struck by the sight of boxes of *soju*, the Korean vodka, just stacked in the street next to a little locked-up shop. No one was around, just a note in the window had the mobile phone number to call the shop assistant if someone wanted to buy.

I won't idealize Korean shopkeepers. Some of them, like shopkeepers in any other country, will be happy to flog some goods at an exorbitant price to an unsuspecting foreigner. Yet I will always remember quite a different example. Once my wife and I, walking along Insadong, Seoul's "souvenir street," bought a small figurine for about 100,000 won (about 100 dollars). I paid with a credit card. In South Korea, credit cards are very popular especially since until recently, the largest banknote was 10,000 won, barely enough to pay for a pair of cheapest cotton pants at a wholesale market, or for a cup of coffee in a five-star hotel. There was a glitch with the card reader, and the shop assistant apologized and swiped the card again. When I received my credit card statement at the end of the month, it turned out, my card had been charged twice. Well, I thought, OK, next time I am on Insadong, I will clear it up with the shop people. But I got swamped with work, next weekend, I was busy with a delegation from Moscow, for the weekend after, I went to Busan. In short, I only managed to come to Insadong about a month and a half after that figurine purchase, and, frankly, I wasn't even quite sure which little shop I had bought it from. So I had to wander around for a bit. And while I was so wandering, the figurine's seller all but jumped me. It felt as if he had been looking for me and my wife in the crowd for the entire month and a half. He nearly forced us to come into his shop, his expressions and gestures were extremely contrite, he tried to explain something, but I could not understand him since I didn't speak Korean, and then he carefully counted off ten notes of 10,000 won each and also gave me a small souvenir plate as a gift.

More serious crimes than a market theft or a picked pocket, felonies like rape or murder, are certainly committed in South Korea, but far more infrequently than in Europe or the US. Consequently, such crimes etch themselves on the collective memory and become surrounded with legend, as in the case of the Hwason serial killer, the most infamous and so far unsolved crime in South Korea. Between 1986 and 1991 in the city of Hwason, ten women were found tied up, raped, and murdered. South Korean police have a remarkable approach to investigating murders. If there is even as much as a hint that a murderer was motivated by financial gain, he or she will be certain to receive the harshest possible sentence.

Organized crime also does exist in South Korea. Yet the mob's interests concentrate on those realms which don't interfere with legal businesses. The mob is involved with prostitution or the underground gambling. One thing that doesn't exist in South Korea is protection rackets. If the poorest shopkeeper is visited by well-muscled and well-armed thugs demanding money "for protection," the police will deal with them rapidly and effectively.

Since life on the Korean Peninsula is still heavily influenced by the military confrontation between the South and the North, South Korea pays great attention to its military. The country has a general conscription law, and men between 19 and 31 must spend two years and two months in active service, and draft dodging is frowned upon. A young man who did not serve in the army might have trouble finding employment, particularly in large and prestigious companies. If, when asked why he didn't serve the young man starts to mumble something to the effect of having been prevented from active service by ill health and mental defect, he will certainly be turned down. The logic behind is that you cannot possibly apply to work in Samsung, LG, or Hyundai, if your health didn't allow you even to stand guard over an army warehouse full of long johns

I am not idealizing the South Korean army service, they have their fair share of problems with draftees; hazing occurs, too, as well as other forms of harassment. Yet most South Koreans I spoke to have good memories of their time in the army and gladly take part in army reunions where drinks flow freely.

On the other hand, high ranking officials who try to dodge rules and obtain release from the army service for their children or to get them placed in a prestigious university or in a cozy place in an organization they supervise will be publicly condemned or even subjected to an administrative punishment should their actions come to light. It happened to one of Korea's Ministers for Foreign Affairs whose daughter was hired by the Ministry in an improper way.

Korean Leaders from a Humble Background

South Korea can boast many stories of amazing success achieved by gifted people who owed their triumph in life not to their social status or sycophantic behavior, but to their willpower, single-mindedness, and diligence. Almost all the leaders in the world of business and politics, people who decide the country's future, are people from humble backgrounds, from poor families with many children, people who experienced privation and hunger.

One of them is Lee Myong-bak, Korea's President in 2008-2013. He was born in 1942 in the Korean neighborhood in Osaka, Japan. He was the fifth of seven children born to the family of an animal farm worker. In 1945, the family decided to move to Korea; the steamer they took sank, taking all their meager possession with it. During the Korean War, little Lee Myong-bak sold matches and scones in the street to help his family. Once he fainted in school due to dystrophy and subsequently was bedridden for four months. Future president swept rubbish at the Itaewon market in Seoul at nights to pay for his university education.

Lee Myong-bak's predecessors, Kim Dae-jung (President in 1998-2003) and Roh Moo-hyun (President in 2003-2008) also came from humble backgrounds. All of them were exceedingly hungry for education. Lee Myong-bak came to politics via business. First, he displayed his talents for leadership in a students' movement, and for many years, he led the construction department of Hyundai. Unlike him, both Kim Dae-jung and Roh Moo-hyun won popular acclaim by participating in democratic movements and opposing authoritarian regimes.

And what about the origins of those people who founded world-famous Korean companies? Most of them were also of humble origins, and some of them didn't even have a high school diploma.

Chung Ju-yung, the founder of Hyundai (Korean for "Modernity"), was born in 1915 to a poor peasant family, one of eight children. After finishing elementary school, future billionaire headed for Seoul to look for work. He did odd jobs, worked as a porter, as a courier, and as an auto mechanic. In 1939, he started his own business, an auto repair shop. In 1946, that shop became the first enterprise bearing the name Hyundai.

Shin Kyuk-ho, the founder of Lotte, came, just like Chung Ju-yung, from a peasant family. He was born in 1922; his parents had ten children, five sons and five daughters. In 1944, he moved to Japan, worked as a porter, as a milkman, but he also managed to graduate from high school and then to graduate from the Waseda university engineering college with a degree in chemistry. Lotte Group was founded in Japan in 1948, and only in 1965, it expanded into Korea. Its name comes from J. W. von Goethe's

The Sorrows of Young Werther. Its heroine Lotte made a lasting impression on Shin Kyuk-ho when he first read the novel. Today, Lotte Group includes 60 companies in Asia, Europe, and America with over 60,000 employees. Its assets are worth about 50 billion dollars. Lotte Group produces candy, it has a fast food chain (Lotteria is the South Korean version of McDonald's), supermarkets and movie theaters, it operates in hotels, insurance, construction, chemical industry, and electronics industry.

In many developing countries of Asia, Africa, and Latin America, a child born to a poor family will never rise to be part of the elite. The developed countries of the West, on the other hand, exhibit the opposite trend: they believe that climbing the ladder of success and rising income is not inherently important. This attitude is widespread in Northern Europe, for instance. Besides, those very countries have a severe progressive taxation system which results in a decreasing gap in incomes between the rich and the poor, and on the whole, the poor lead a relatively comfortable and quiet life. The career ladder in those countries exists for the ambitious and mercenary minority, and the majority are satisfied with their life as it is and they don't expend efforts on social climbing. Koreans themselves often speak about inequality which allegedly exists in their society. However, compared to other countries with similar levels of income, South Korea can boast a high level of financial equality and a high social mobility. A South Korean boy or girl from a poor family can have a stellar career and join the ranks of the political and business elite. However, having a diploma from one of the top-ten or top-twenty universities is a *conditio sine qua non* for getting one's foot on the first rung of that social ladder.

Testing Hell

South Korea has a cult of education. Most South Korean school students call their high school graduation year "a year of hell." That year, they take the "Great Test," the College Scholastic Ability Test (CSAT). Since their test results ultimately determine the university they can enroll in, and consequently, their entire future life, the Test is no trifling matter.

South Korean teenagers spent 7.6 hours on average at school each day, and then several more hours in the so-called cram schools, classes with private tutors. Wishing to alleviate the financial burden of those cram schools, Lee Myong-Bak's administration prohibited holding private tutoring sessions after 10 pm. Special inspectors monitor compliance with that prohibition.

Psychological burden in schools results in a large number of suicides among students. Presidential Advisory Council on Education, Science and Technology reports that 200 students committed suicide in 2009, and 150 in 2010.

The Great Test includes four mandatory subjects and three elective subjects. The history of Korea, the Korean language, English, and math are mandatory.

The Great Test is usually conducted in November. On November 7, 2013, 650,000 students simultaneously took the test in 1,257 testing centers throughout South Korea. That day, the entire police staff and transportation employees were all on duty, with time-off and vacations cancelled. The opening hour in several governmental bodies and businesses was pushed an hour forward to reduce the traffic load; traffic was limited within 200 meters of all the testing centers; flights were cancelled between 1:10 and 1:40 pm to make sure students would have no problem getting to those testing centers for which school facilities were used. For a few weeks before the Test, churches and Buddhist temples were packed with people, mostly women, who prayed for their children's success (Korean journalists love to take pictures of these women as living symbols of Korean mothers' dedication to their families). However, it seems to me that those Koreans who succumb to the testing fever (also called "testing hell") apparently miss the fact that this fever is linked to those traits of the Korean society which the Koreans themselves are quite proud of. In particular, testing fever reflects the cult of social mobility which is widespread in today's South Korea, and it also reflects the fact that social mobility in South Korea indeed exists.

Justice the Korean Way

Korean society, just like any other, has its notions of justice: the correlation between action and reaction, rights and obligations, crime and punishment. Naturally, this correlation isn't always perfect. South Korea has its share of corruption, abuse of power, and direct breaching of the law. Under former military regimes, the rulers weren't particularly concerned about punishment for their unsavory actions, believing they would get away scot-free, but after the democratic changes in the late 1980s - early 1990s, the situation started to change.

In 1992, South Korea elected its first civil president since 1961, Kim Young-sam, a member of the opposition. Since his predecessors have already carried out principal democratic reforms in the country, Kim Young-sam focused on domestic issues, and particularly on fighting corruption. Several ministers, high ranking officials, parliament deputies, members of the military were forced to resign, and some even found themselves behind bars.

However, those hit the hardest were Kim Young-sam's predecessors in the office of the president: generals Chun Doo-hwan and Roh Tae-woo. At the trial held in 1995, they were charged with everything from trampling rights and freedoms to cruel suppression of student uprisings and torture of political prisoners. After a lengthy trial, Chun Doo-hwan was sentenced to death (later the sentence was commuted to a life sentence), and Roh Tae-woo was sentenced to twenty two and a half years in prison. However, neither general stayed in prison for too long. In 1998, they were pardoned by the newly-elected president Kim Dae-jung who had been in opposition fighting against the military regime. Kim Dae-jung was dubbed "Asia's Mandela," he spent more than fifteen years in prison, he was twice sentenced to death, he survived several assassination attempts organized by Korean secret services. Both Chun Doo-hwan and Roh Tae-woo are still alive, they are interviewed from time and time and sometimes can even be spotted at official ceremonies.

Many of South Korea's leading businessmen also have their issues with the law. When in 1999, Daewoo, the-then second largest conglomerate in South Korea, which had invested in around 100 countries, went bankrupt after the Asian financial crisis and was left with 90 billion dollars in debt, its chairman Kim Woo-choong fled to France. He came back to Korea in June of 2005 after six years abroad, and was soon arrested and charged with fraud in the amount of 43.4 billion dollars, with illegally borrowing 10.3 billion dollars, and with illegally draining 3.2 billion dollars from the country. In May 2006, he was sentenced to ten years, but was amnestied in December 2007 by the liberal president Roh Moo-hyun.

In 2006, Chung Mong-koo, head of Hyundai-KIA Motor Group, was also embroiled in a huge scandal. He was found guilty of starting an illegal fund used to siphon over 100 million dollars off from the company. Three quarters of that money Chung spent on his personal needs and on bribing governmental officials. Prosecution asked for a six-year prison sentence, claiming that a softer sentence would damage the country image in fighting corruption. The media started a campaign in Chung Mong-koo's defense. They extolled his achievements in strengthening Korea's economy, praised his generous charity donations, emphasized the ill health of the sixty eight-year-old businessman. It was rather funny to watch on television a large, robust man, looking somehow like Yeltsin in the best of times, being wheeled into court in a wheelchair. The court initially sentenced Chung Mong-koo to three years in prison, but South Korea's Supreme Court commuted the sentence to probation. As the Chief Justice explained, when making the decision he felt it necessary to take into account not only Chung Mong-koo's trespasses, but "several other considerations as well." Wheelchair was no longer seen in Chung Mong-koo's photos. In August 2011, world's top news agencies reported that Chung Mong-koo, chairman of the Hyundai-KIA Motor Group, gave 500 billion won (464 million dollars) of his own money to charity, a record amount for South Korea. The money was given to the charity Chung Mong-koo founded in 2007 to help children from poor families receive education.

Lee Kun-hee, the chairman of Samsung and the richest man in Korea, had his brush with the law, too. His fortune is estimated to be 8.73 trillion won, or about 8 billion dollars. He was the head of Samsung for two decades, and it was largely due to him that an average company became one of the largest industrial financial groups in the world. In April 2008, pressured with charges of tax evasion and business ethics breaching, Lee Kun-hee was forced to resign. However, six months later, the Supreme Court dismissed most charges and sentenced him to three-year probation and a fine of 90 million dollars. The fine was paid, and the probation was repealed under Presidential amnesty. Two years later, Lee Kun-hee returned to Samsung as head of Samsung Electronics, the group's leading company.

Chey Tae-wong, chairman of SK, South Korea's largest oil refinery, the son of the company's founder and son-in-law of former president Roh Tae-woo, was sentenced to a three-year prison term for multibillion dollar securities fraud. However, he was released after three months in prison.

South Korea, like other countries, doesn't abandon its own. But it's not only the matter of covering each other's backs. Koreans care not so much about a severe punishment, as about a public shaming of a person who has committed a crime. The society pointed out the person's guilt, he or she admitted their guilt, and then they have to square it with their conscience.

At the same time, Koreans have a particularly sharp sense of injustice. I will quote two incidents that took place while I was working in South Korea.

In February 2008, a sixty-nine-year-old man by name of Chae Jong-gi torched ancient ceremonial gate Namdemun in downtown Seoul. When he was arrested, it turned out he had been arrested two years ago for the attempt to set on fire the imperial palace in Seoul, but he had been released due to his advanced age and because his attempt had failed. Chae, however, was no ordinary pyromaniac. By his own admission, he attempted his crimes because of his grievances against the city administration. City reconstruction affected his house. He was paid a compensation, but he deemed it insufficient, and to avenge what he thought was an injustice done to him, he burned down one of the country's cultural treasures.

The other incident is far more tragic. In 2004-2008, Roh Moo-hyun, a liberal and a former human rights activist, was president of South Korea. I believe him to have been an honest and conscionable person, maybe even an idealist, and I always found him to have a very attractive personality. He actively sought to bring two Koreas closer together. In 2007, he even traveled by car to Pyongyang to meet North Korea's leader Kim Jong-il. By the time his term in office ended, Roh Moo-hyun, despite his best efforts, had a very low approval rating. I won't attempt to explain this development since it would take too detailed an excursion into Korea's domestic and foreign politics. However, Roh Moo-hyun was noticeably upset with such an unfavorable conclusion of his political career. Having moved out of the presidential palace, he settled in his native village in the southern mountains, and, dressed like every other peasant there and wearing a large-brimmed straw hat, he spent his time bicycling around and talking life with anyone who dropped by, oftentimes with complete strangers. This serene life in retirement was suddenly interrupted by a subpoena to appear before an investigative body in Seoul where Roh Moo-hyun was charged with accepting a six-million-dollar bribe. Roh Moo-hyun's and his wife's explanation that those six million dollars had been borrowed from friends to buy a house for their son were deemed unconvincing, and investigators continued to subpoena Roh Moo-hyun to attend hours-long interrogations which sometimes went well past midnight.

To protest such treatment and to prove his innocence, Roh Moo-hyun committed suicide on May 23, 2009 by jumping off a cliff not far from his house. The news of their former president's suicide shocked the country and caused an unprecedented wave of compassion. Over a few hours, hundreds of altars were erected in the streets throughout South Korea, bearing Roh Moo-hyun's portraits. Tens of thousands of people brought flowers and prayed there. Roh Moo-hyun was given full ceremonial burial with presidential honors, and the day of his funeral was truly a day of national mourning.

Diplomatic Corps In Seoul

The diplomatic corps in Seoul is very large, which is only to be expected given South Korea's current economical weight. There is another reason for it, too: given the unrelenting confrontation with North Korea, South Koreans are interested in having the largest possible number of embassies, as if striving to prove their advantage over Pyongyang.

South Korea gives foreign diplomats every opportunity to acquaint the residents of Seoul with their respective cultures, cuisines, tourist attractions. For instance, on the City Day which is celebrated annually on the first or second Sunday of May, one of the central streets is closed off for traffic and the so-called diplomatic bazaar is set up there. Each of the hundred embassies sets up its pavilion, decorated with flags and posters, where ambassadors' wives and sometimes ambassadors themselves offer samples of national cuisine and drinks their countries are famous for; some offer tequila, some vodka, some wine or beer. For a charge, of course. Souvenirs are sold there, too. Special music venues are offered for amateur musical performances by embassy personnel. There are drawing competitions held among children attending embassy schools, etc.

The Russian pavilion always drew crowds, and not only because we offered vodka and crepes with caviar and salmon, pickled cucumbers, Russian pies and kebabs hot off the spit, sold matryoshkas, Gzhel ceramics, and Pavlovo-Posad shawls which are hugely popular in Korea. We had the most beautiful girls and young staff talking to guests in good Korean, which gave the locals a pleasant surprise.

The bazaar was always visited by the Mayor of Seoul, by the City Council's deputies, other eminent politicians, who would gladly have a friendly drink with their hosts at a celebration for which you didn't need passes or entrance tickets, a celebration attended by tens of thousands of locals who came with their families, with children and friends.

In the fall, Seoul International Women's Association held its annual bazaars. That was an event organized on a smaller scale, but it also included music, songs, dances and it was very popular among Seoul women.

The most elite event in the informal social life of the diplomatic corps in Seoul was the annual Parade of Nations. It was a grand banquet and concert, with proceeds going to charity. Entry tickets cost up to 200 dollars, and it was supposed to be a black-tie event, even though not many attendees complied with that requirement. Cream of the crop of South Korean business was in attendance, and the Minister of Foreign Affairs was the traditional guest of honor.

The Parade of Nations was organized by ambassadors' wives headed by the Doyen's spouse. A committee would be formed. They rented the grand hall of one of Seoul's most prestigious hotels, usually of the Hyatt. The committee members would make a list of what each embassy could contribute, from money to a couple of cases of alcohol, or some art objects for the raffle.

The event attracted many sponsors, foreign businesses working in Seoul or South Korean companies wishing to move into foreign markets. I particularly remember a Korean firm which produced some mushroom infusion for treating hangover. Upon leaving the banquet, each guest received a nicely packed set of bottles with this mysterious potion.

I also remember a very interesting concert. Personnel from the Côte d'Ivoire Embassy with their teenage children wearing national feather-decorated clothes rocked the stage with a flamboyant African dance. A pair from Argentine danced the tango, the American ambassador played percussion with a Korean jazz band, Belgian ambassador played some incredible wind instrument, and the husband of New Zealand's lady ambassador, a black New Yorker, performed blues, while Indian ambassador's wife performed Bharatnatyam, a classical Indian dance.

Russian performers invariably garnered ovations. A. Svyatkin, music professor at a prestigious university, wowed the audience with his inspired piano playing. Our school's dancing studio performed an almost professional quadrille, and Kristina Khoreva, a high school student, sang Russian hits, charming the audience not so much with her voice and professionalism, as with her youthful spontaneity and charisma.

Our school's amateur performers were in general very popular in Seoul. I remember Ban Ki-moon, South Korea's long-time Minister for Foreign Affairs wishing to bid farewell to the Seoul diplomatic corps before departing to assume his new office in New York. A week before the banquet I received a call from South Korea's Ministry of Foreign Affairs, they wanted someone from our embassy to take part in the evening's concert program. I agreed, and we were the only foreign performers, everybody else was from the Korean Ministry of Foreign Affairs. The daughter of our embassy's counselor together with a Korean girl who also went to our embassy school sang a famous Soviet song "A Million of Scarlet Roses," each of them singing in her native language, in Russian and Korean respectively. The faces of Ban Ki-moo and his wife at that moment are still a precious memory.

André Kim, an Haute Couture Designer

Foreign ambassadors in Seoul took part in many other cultural events and functions. I would like to specifically mention fashion shows by South Korea's leading designer André Kim who sadly passed away. When I made his acquaintance, he was already over seventy, but he was a very vibrant and artistic person. André Kim was the first person in South Korea to go into haute couture. André Kim started his career in the early 1960s and made a name for himself and for his country. The French Figaro once called André Kim "a magician from the land of dreams." Kim had his fashion shows in Paris, New York, Singapore, Shanghai, and many other cities around the globe. International Olympic Committee invited him to be the stage director of the Olympic opening ceremonies in Barcelona and Atlanta. André Kim's name became a brand, a symbol of romantic elegance. He designed clothes, jewelry, porcelain, wall paper, various household articles, and even credit cards.

Unfortunately, Moscow never saw an André Kim fashion show. I spared no efforts to organize such a show, but I ran into the unbreakable barrier of Moscow's peculiar show business, which would be out of place to describe here. And André Kim was very fond of Russia. All his shows invariably started with the powerful bars of Tchaikovsky's Piano Concerto # 1, and the majority of his models were Russian.

André Kim gave a lot to charity, and each year, proceeds from one of his shows were donated to UNICEF, the UN's Children's Foundation. Kim had the idea to engage foreign ambassadors and their wives as model for his UNICEF-benefiting evenings. Ambassadors or ambassadors' wives from the Netherlands, Israel, Denmark, China, South Africa, Germany, France, New Zealand, agreed, as did yours truly and my wife. Needless to say, shows with such participants had record-breaking attendance and profits.

On Vodka and On Taxes

Robert Owen, a utopian thinker, believed that the foremost right of a working person is the right to knock down a shot of cheap and good quality vodka after a day of hard work. In South Korea, this idea was put into practice. Korean vodka *soju* is sold everywhere, in small bottles not unlike Pepsi or Coke bottles, without any time limits. Standard mass-produced *soju* is about

35 proof, although some premium kinds can be about 70 proof. A bottle of standard *soju* costs about one dollar, which is very cheap by South Korean standards, especially given the average wages in the country.

So, are the Koreans being driven to alcoholism? Naturally, low priced *soju* isn't conducive to people being teetotalers. Koreans do drink, and they drink a lot, the young generation drinks, too, including girls, but I believe that the availability of low-priced alcohol means no one dies of counterfeit booze as happens in Russia and in India where alcohol sales are strictly limited in many ways. No one produces counterfeit liquor, nobody flogs it to local alcoholics. It would bring no profit. There is a list of companies licensed to produce *soju*, and everybody knows their brands.

But what about excise duties, doesn't Korea's state budget lose a significant share of profits? No, it does not. Money comes not from excise duties on alcohol, that is, not from the poor, but from more affluent people. Money comes in due to progressive taxation system, due to high importing duties on luxury items such as furs, jewelry, designer clothing bought by the rich, due to excise duties on premium alcohol, such as vintage wines, premium whiskeys and cognacs bought by the rich, and not by working stiffs.

No one would deny that South Korea is a democratic country with a market economy, but Korea is not shy about taxing its fat cats. Income tax is 6 per cent for people with annual income below 12 million won (12,000 dollars), and up to 35 per cent for those who make more than 88 million won (88,000 dollars) a year.

South Korea is a member of the World Trade Organization (WTO), but it firmly protects its industry and agriculture from foreign competition. You will rarely see a foreign-made car or bus in Korea. There are lots of vehicles of all sorts, but 99 per cent are Korean-made: Hyundai, KIA, Ssanyoung, Renault Samsung, or Daewoo (the automotive company was acquired by General Motors). The reason is simple. A 25 per cent import duty must be paid on foreign-made compact cars. For high-end cars, this duty goes up to 30 per cent. Thus, domestic market is protected from foreign-made cars, and Korea's own automotive industry receives a serious boost.

The government also protects Korean farmers. They believe that the spirit of the nation is preserved by the peasants, and for peasants to survive, they must be supported. Therefore, South Korea has very high import duties on rice, vegetables, fruit, meat. For instance, import duty on pork is up to 25 per cent, on beef, up to 40 per cent.

"Korean Economic Miracle" and Its Makers

South Koreans have every reason to be proud of their country; stricken with abject poverty and nearly laid waste by war in the early 1950s, over the life-span of a single generation, it became a highly developed prosperous state (the per capita GDP grew from USD 100 in 1963 to over USD 22.4 thousand in 2012).

The methods which allowed to achieve this impressive economic breakthrough squarely refute our Russian liberals who like to yak on and on that an economic breakthrough is only possible in an unregulated market.

The "Korean economic miracle" was wrought by general Park Chung-hee. He came to power after a military coup in May 1961. Starting with him, for thirty years Korea was ruled by generals.

Park Chung-hee's predecessor left him a miserable legacy: during the tenure of Syng Man Rhee, Korea's first president, who ruled with an iron hand from 1948 until 1960, more than a half of the country's budget and more than two thirds of its military expenditure were covered by economic aid from the US, and virtually all economic indicators put North Korea ahead of South Korea.

Park Chung-hee started to modernize Korea, at the same time cruelly suppressing any democratic leanings. Since South Korea had very limited natural resources and an overabundance of cheap labor, the decision was made to follow the export-oriented model. The main question, though, was who would put this model into practice. Most South Korean businesses at that point were small enterprises engaged either in manufacturing some of the simplest household items or in agricultural processing. They had neither the finances nor the experience of working with foreign clients and could not even dream of moving into the international market.

So Park Chung-hee handpicked several dozen businesses that appeared to him to have the greatest potential, and the principal criterion was not so much their business as such, as the personal qualities of their owners. Dictator Park Chung-hee proceeded on Stalin's principle that "the human factor is all-important," and his approach turned out to be the correct one. The businesses included in the list received direct support from the state, all kinds of preferences, they had preferential access to loans and foreign investments. So ultimately, by the late 1970s, there were fifteen conglomerate industrial groups, the so-called Chaebol, including such famous ones as Samsung, Hyundai, LG, etc.

In 1962, South Korea adopted its first five-year economic development plan with a program for developing the industrial sector, and its export-oriented nature was supported by close ties with the US. Before South Korea started to raise wages sharply in the mid-1980s, the country mostly produced consumer goods for foreign consumers. In 1969, when Samsung started making black-and-white TVs, only 2 per cent of Koreans had a TV.

In 1965, large-scale construction started, and the first prefab four-storey apartment building, without elevators, was erected. In 1970, the Seoul-Busan highway (428 kilometers) became operational. Its construction marked a watershed in South Korea's transportation infrastructure development. In 1974, Seoul subway started operating, replacing the system of streetcars which existed since the early 20th century. Building the new, modern Seoul which is a deserved point of pride for today's South Koreans, involved significant difficulties and even some disasters. Among them, the partial collapse of the Seongsu Bridge across the Hangan river in Seoul on October 21, 1994, and the Sampoong Department Store collapse on June 29, 1995 were the most notorious. 22 people died in the bridge collapse, and 501 in the department store collapse.

Gradually, small and medium businesses grew in number and significance, and leading offices in the governmental bodies were given to technocrats who had been educated abroad. Annual economic growth reached 9.2 per cent, export grew by 32.8 per cent, and the per capita GDP grew from 87 dollars in 1962 to 1,053 dollars in 1980. By 1971, South Korea's budget no longer depended on the US economic aid.

In 1971, the president initiated the "For the New Countryside" program. The government poured money into agriculture, into road-building and residential construction in the country, and it resulted in countryside poverty finally abating. In 1965, average income of a peasant family was only 423 dollars, in 1971 it was 1,025 dollars, and in 1977, it reached 2,960 dollars, that is, it grew nearly sevenfold over twelve years. The increase in purchasing power in the countryside led to a sharp increase in demand for construction materials, fertilizers, agricultural machinery, home appliances, in its turn spurring subsequent increases in manufacturing.

Every decade, South Korea introduced additional modifications and nuances into its industrial policies. In the early 1960s, the emphasis was on developing legislation to regulate export. In the 1970s, the emphasis was on heavy and chemical industries, in the 1980s, on developing small and medium businesses, in 1990s, on liberalizing the market, and starting in the year 2000, South Korea pays special attention to industry innovation, including interactions between small, medium, and large businesses.

The history of principal Chaebol illustrates the development of South Korea's industry and its diversification.

For instance, Lee Byung-chull, the founder of Samsung Group (in Korean, it means "three stars"), started out in 1930s selling rice flour and dried fish. During the Korean War, he started manufacturing rice vodka and beer which he supplied to the allied forces. Several years later, Lee Byung-chull founded a textile manufacture. After Syng Man Rhee was overthrown in 1960, all of Lee Byung-chull's assets were confiscated, and he was jailed for bribery. Only by the late 1960s, Lee Byung-chull had achieved permanent success; he had gone into electronics manufacturing and established Samsung as a world-famous brand. Today, Samsung manufactures everything from microwave ovens and toasters to digital cameras and stereo systems, from cars to ocean ships and planes. For the domestic market, Samsung develops some military vehicles; it is also engaged in finances, insurance, hotel business, and security services, and is the source of over 50 per cent of South Korea's budget. It employs almost 300,000 people across the globe, and in 2010, its income after taxes was just a little short of 15 billion dollars.

I have already mentioned that Hyundai started as an auto repair shop. In 1947, its founder Chung Ju-yung started a construction business with the same name. Further on, particularly at the time of the Korean War, Chung Ju-yung was greatly helped by his younger brother who had learned English in Japan. At that time, very few people in Korea spoke English, and his brother's fluency allowed Chung Ju-yung to establish close ties with Americans who commissioned many construction projects. As a result, by the late 1950s, Hyundai was a prosperous business. In the 1960s, it went into construction abroad, first in Vietnam and in the countries of Southeast Asia where it built military facilities for Americans, and then in the Middle East where in 1970s, South Korean construction companies were particularly active. Hyundai had a lot of construction projects in South Korea itself. When the government concentrated on heavy industry in 1970s, Hyundai contributed, too. In 1973, it inaugurated Hyundai Heavy Industries shipbuilding wharf in Ulsan, which managed to get some lucrative foreign custom. In 1974, the first South Korean supertanker *The Atlantic Baron* with the displacement of 267,000 tons was launched. At the same time, they started building Hyundai Motors car manufacturing plants. In 1975, they manufactured the first car fully made in South Korea, and by 1990, South Korea had gained a position among the world's leading car manufacturers. In the early 1980s, Korea started manufacturing electronics, and Hyundai Group again was among the trailblazers. Hyundai Electronics founded in 1983 (today the company is called Hynix) gradually became one of the world' leading semiconductor manufacturers.

Koo In Hwoi, founder of LG Corporation (formerly Lucky Goldstar, now Life's Good), started out in 1947 with a small cosmetics business. A couple of years later, besides making creams and tooth pastes, the company started making cream jars and tooth paste tubes from imported plastics, and in 1952, it became the first South Korean plastics manufacturer. Then they started making plastic cases for radios and various household appliances, and then proceeded to make radios and appliances themselves. In 1959, they made the first South Korean radio, in 1960, the first fan, the first telephone in 1961, the first fridge in 1965, the first washing machine in 1969, the first color TV in 1976, and the first video camera in 1981. In 2009, LG Corporation turnover was about 80 billion dollars, its profit was 1.2 billion dollars, and they employed 186,000 people.

The Chaebol are family holdings, and top positions in those companies are usually held by members of the same family, which gives liberal economists grounds for criticism. Besides, the Chaebol would hardly have been just as successful without the state's constant support.

The South Korean economic model is still not free from state regulation. Yet far from decreasing the economy's efficiency, this regulation constantly increases it and guarantees both stable general growth and the improvement of quality of life. Average wages calculated in purchasing power parity (32,638 dollars in 2009, or about 2,170 dollars a month) is only slightly lower than in Japan (32,816 dollars) and in Spain (32,957 dollars), and it is higher than in Italy (32,121 dollars). And we are speaking about average wages for the country; highly qualified workers in leading industries, for instance, in shipbuilding or in power engineering industry make 5-6 thousand dollars a month. In 2010, human development index put South Korea # 12 in the world. It earned high marks on three indicators, with health care system being the highest, and wages level being the lowest.

Russia and Korea

What is the attitude to Russia and Russians in South Korea? I can openly state that there is no official or popular Russophobia, and not because South Koreans are committed to some sort of political correctness. When they are displeased with some foreign state's policies, they declare their displeasure fairly openly.

Let's take a telltale example: picketing foreign embassies. Judge for yourselves: the Embassy of the US, South Korea's principal strategic ally, is located on Seoul's main thoroughfare, and it is always tightly cordoned off by police buses and police units in full state-of-the-art riot gear. It is because this embassy is picketed often and very energetically, too.

The Embassy of Japan is heavily protected, too. The narrow side street where the embassy is located is always blocked with police buses. People often picket the embassy, shouting anti-Japanese slogans, demanding that Japan apologize for using Korean girls as sex slaves during World War II, or protesting Japan's claims to the Korean island of Tokto.

The Chinese have built a magnificent embassy where the Taiwan embassy used to be. Unfortunately, I haven't seen it yet. Yet I remember two police buses permanently parked by the old Chinese embassy which was regularly picketed by members of the Falun Gong sect which is proscribed in China.

The Russian Embassy had a standard police booth at the entrance with a single police officer on duty. During more than four years of my work in Seoul, only once a group of no more than seven people approached the Embassy, produced a picketing permit issued by the local authorities, and then spent about an hour standing quietly by the gate, holding a little poster in support of some prisoner in Russia of whom I knew nothing.

Geographically, Russia and Korea are neighbors. Yet for a long time, Korea was overshadowed by China and remained closed for foreigners. The Russia-Korea border was determined in 1861 along with the Russia-China border after the Ussuri territory covering the area between the Amur and the Ussuri rivers and the Sea of Japan was united with Russia. Anyhow the state-to-state relations with Korea were established by Russia in 1884 only at the same time with Germany, Britain, France and the USA, after Korea had been opened for international contacts.

So the history of bilateral Russian-Korean relations is a little over 150 years. In 1890-s the Russian presence in Seoul was quite visible. The first European style hotel was started in the city by Ms.Sontag, the sister-in-law of the Russian envoy. Russian architect A.Sabatin took part in designing and constructing the new building of the Royal residence in the Deoksagung Palace compound, ajacent to the Russian legation, and the Myendong Catholic Cathedral, the most remarkable building of Seoul of that period. A Russian Orthodox church was opened in Seoul in 1903.

Russian diplomats played an influential role in Seoul. The then Korean King Gojong made a serious stake at Russia's support in resisting the Japanese invasion to Korea. After in 1895 his wife Empress Myeongseong (referred to as "*Queen Min*" by the Japanese) was assassinated by Japanese agents, King Gojong and his crown prince fled from the palace to the Russian legation in Seoul, from which they governed for about one year, an event known as Korea royal refuge at the Russian legation. The growing Russian presence in Korea was used by the Japanese as a pretext to start the war with Russia in 1904.

The short period of Russia-Korea rapprochement at the turn of 19th-20th centuries was followed by a long period of mutual isolation, which for South Korea lasted until 1990. In 1910, Japan annexed Korea and it didn't merely close Korea's door on Russia, the Japanese consistently kept persuading Koreans that their northern neighbor is a naturally aggressive, expansionist state populated with rough, cruel, and immoral people, and therefore, Russia is Korea's long-standing enemy.

Dr. Lee In-ho, an eminent Korean Slavist, former South Korean ambassador to Russia, once told me a telltale example. In 1906 or 1907, when her grandmother was six, she was enrolled in a Japanese kindergarten. The first song Japanese teachers taught to the Korean children was the song of General Kuropatkin being the most evil person in the world (Kuropatkin commanded Russian troops during the Russo-Japanese War of 1904-1905).

In the universities the Japanese opened in Korea, in the newspapers and books they published for Koreans, the Japanese consistently claimed that had not Japan annexed Korea, Korea would have been conquered by Russia, and it would have been much, much worse for the Koreans.

The Russophobic propaganda perpetrated by the Japanese a hundred years ago has, unfortunately, proved to be quite tenacious. Some echoes can still be heard in the works of some South Korean historians, although historical evidence irrefutably states that Russia never strove for any domination in Korea, and never had any plans to annex it and make it part of the Russian Empire. In the 1920s-1930s, the Japanese propaganda added a hammer, a sickle and a red star to its stock image of the evil Russian bear baring its fangs to threaten its neighbors. If the Imperial Russia was simply a "threat from the North," the Soviet Union was depicted as the vehicle for the "Communist menace" which Tokyo deemed to be far more dangerous.

The Soviet Union played the key role in liberating Korea from the Japanese colonial yoke in 1945, and it resulted in a wave of pro-Soviet sentiments in Korea. Yet in its southern part, the right-wing anti-communist politicians and American occupation authorities did their best to eradicate any good feelings toward Russia. In 1950, the Korean War started, the USSR sided with the North, and for forty years, until the late 1980s, the Soviet Union, Russia, and Moscow were taboo for South Koreans. Any contacts, correspondence, Soviet newspapers and magazines were prohibited.

Frankly speaking, the Soviet side discouraged, to put it mildly, contacts with South Korea, particularly with South Korean officials as well. Our North Korean comrades played a great part in it. I remember my first diplomatic posting to Delhi in the 1970s. At a grand reception, some western colleague, as if accidentally, introduces to you an Oriental-looking person dressed in a typical European suit. "Meet my Korean friend." The Korean friend is smiling pleasantly. The "friend" is clearly from Seoul, because comrades from Pyongyang all wear Mao jackets with badges with Kim Il-sung's portrait. But what can you do? You cannot just turn your back on him, especially since the South Korean has already offered his hand to shake. So you shake hands and then take your leave. And next day, the Minister-Councellor or even the Ambassador himself reprimands you: "Yesterday at the reception you talked to a person from the South Korean embassy. You do know the Soviet Union has no diplomatic relations with that country. So I strongly recommend that in the future, you refrain from such contacts." Things are crystal clear: nothing slipped under the all-seeing eye of our comrades from the North Korean Embassy, they spotted me shaking hands with the South Korean and, naturally, snitched on me.

Despite the absence of official contacts, Russian culture made its way into South Korea even at the time of the Japanese occupation, and, paradoxically, it did so via Japan. Koreans studying in Japan or keeping touch with Japanese intellectuals, learned about Tchaikovsky's music, Stanislavsky's method acting, Russian ballet (starting with Anna Pavlova's 1922 tour of Japan, the Japanese became hugely interested in classical choreography), but principally, they familiarized themselves with the great Russian literature. They read Japanese translations of Tolstoy, Chekhov, Dostoevsky; those books were translated into Korean from Japanese because there were no translators from Russian in Korea. Shin Kyok-ho, founder of Lotte Group whom I have already mentioned, had started his business in Japan, and being already well advanced in years, he told me about the great impression made upon him by Dostoevsky's novels which he had read in Japanese in his youth.

Elderly South Korean university professors remembered nostalgically the late 1950s-early 1960s, when they secretly passed to each other Maxim Gorky's novel *Mother* and gathered to listen to the old Russian song "Stenka Razin" with its story of the leader of a major peasant rebellion in the 17th century. They thought it to be the most revolutionary of songs, and they sang along, even without understanding the Russian words.

In the 1960s-1970s, some South Koreans went to the UK or the US to study Russian, first Russian language departments appeared in South Korean universities, South Korean presses began to publish classical Russian literature, and even some Soviet literature in Korean translations.

The first significant contact between the Soviet people and the South Koreans took place during 1988 Seoul Olympics. At that point, the USSR didn't look like "the evil empire" to South Koreans; they no longer thought of it mostly in terms South Korean and American propaganda which depicted the USSR as a Communist dinosaur, bristling with ballistic missiles and pumping Pyongyang military muscles.

Our country was surrounded with the halo of perestroika, glasnost, new thinking, and pluralism, the circumlocutional Gorbachev hugging the top anti-communist Reagan was a frequent sight on TV. And South Korea of the Olympics was a different country, too. It was a more democratic country, shaking off the shackles of military dictatorships. Soviet athletes came to a modern, clean, and bright city full of smiling, welcoming people. Both in Moscow and in Seoul, people were convinced that our two countries, having left behind their authoritarian past, Communist and anti-Communist respectively, can proceed to a new stage of good neighborly relations and close cooperation based on their mutual commitment to the ideals of democracy.

And after the establishment of diplomatic relations between the Soviet Union and Korea on September 30, 1990, our bilateral exchanges boomed. There was a steady stream of economic and public delegations coming to Seoul from Moscow, Soviet artists toured South Korea for the first time, and South Korean businessmen and students, especially those who wanted to study ballet, opera, and drama traveled to Moscow. The expectations were great.

Yet the Soviet Union desintegrated, and hard times befell Russia. Foreign trade legislation was amended nearly every month, forcing new negotiations on previously concluded contracts. South Korean businessmen, used to dealing with respectable, reliable partners, in the newly democratic Russia, especially in the provinces, encountered people who never fulfilled their obligations and, moreover, took every chance to con their partners, and there was no way to bring them to justice. Now Seoul and Pusan were visited by a steady stream of rogues of all kinds; a lot of them came from the Far East which was conveniently nearby, and they traded in illegally obtained timber and fish. It was those characters that average South Koreans encountered in their everyday life, and it was them, and not Tolstoy's and Chekhov's characters who shaped, at least for some time, the Koreans' image of a "typical Russian." And that image was not far removed both from the image of "northern barbarians" popularized by the Japanese, and from the image of Russians as halfwits, thieves, and thugs typical for American movies and today Russian TV shows.

It took a lot of time and effort to change the negative image of Russia and Russians in South Korea. Even the large South Korean companies interested in developing partnerships with Russia, moved into the Russian market again only in 2002-2003, when they became convinced that Vladimir Putin as President of Russia controlled the situation in the country.

And it is the colossal achievement of our musicians, actors, and athletes, that they managed to create a human image of Russia for the South Korean society. The best shows of the Korean National Ballet were directed by Yuri Grigorovitch, the chief director of the Bolshoi Ballet of Moscow, and those of the "Universal ballet" by Oleg Vinogradov, the former head of the world known Mariinsky Ballet of St.Petersburg. Many of South Korean singers, ballet dancers, classical musicians who studied in Moscow and St. Petersburg, also popularize Russian culture in South Korea.

Yet classical art is mostly popular among the elite. As far as average South Koreans, and particularly children, are concerned, for them Russia is mostly associated with our famous trio of figure skaters, Natalya Bestemyanova, Igor Bobrin, and Andrey Bukin. Their ice show is an annual event in all main South Korean cities.

In South Korea's market society, we sometimes have to promote Russian culture using some sort of "brands." For instance, very few people in Korea ever heard about Russian painters. And when we organized the first ever exhibition of Russian art from the collections of the Russian Museum and the Tretyakov Gallery, Koreans insisted that we call it "Kandinsky and Masterpieces of Russian Art," and not just "Masterpieces of Russian Art." They said that Kandinsky is a world-famous brand, and only his name will guarantee us success. We had to agree, and the exhibition was, indeed, a smashing success. For as long as the exhibition was on, Koreans stood in the never-ending line to get into Seoul Arts Center, and thanks to Kandinsky, they also saw paintings by other classical artists, bought lots of albums and postcards, and also scarves and caps with the exhibition logo, carefully prepared by the Korean organizers.

The paleontological exhibition from Russian museums organized in 2007 was also done on heavily commercial lines. We brought many skeletons of dinosaurs and other exotic animals, including Dima the baby mammoth, the only fully preserved mammoth in the world, discovered in the North of Yakutia. Koreans thronged to see the exhibition. Dima carried the day, its photographs and souvenir figurines, as well as plastic sets of dinosaur bones to assemble as a sort of jigsaw puzzle were sold like hot pies.

South Koreans have long been treating Russian songs "Cranes" and "Million of Scarlet Roses" like their own. Some of our current pop hits are popular, too. I think it is due to the fact that even though the Russian text of today's hits is usually pathetic, they have fairly melodious tunes. Unlike, for instance, American rap, it is somehow similar to the Korean melodies. In 2006-2008, Russian and Korean Russian language instructors from Kemyong University in the city of Daegu initiated the all-Korean competition for the best performance of a modern Russian pop song; this competition is annually attended by competitors from no less than 15 South Korean universities where Russian is taught.

As far as Russian sports are concerned, Russian beauties Elena Isinbaeva and Maria Sharapova are very popular in South Korea, but the true hero among the Korean youth is Fedor Emelianenko, mixed martial arts champion. I could personally see that his name is third famous in South Korea, immediately following Vladimir Putin and Dmitry Medvedev. Due to Fedor's (as he is known) fame, *sambo*, the Russian martial art, is gaining popularity in Korea. *Sambo* classes are open in most cities and provinces, and Korea's National Sambo Federation headed by Moon Chon-geum, a very energetic president, became a kind of Korean-Russian friendship society.

Who Stalin, Khrushchev, and Brezhnev Were

It should be said, though, that most South Koreans know very little about Russia, and their knowledge is rather superficial, being based mostly on the ideological clichés churned out by CNN, BBC, and other centers of western propaganda. Today, these clichés travel from country to country. Russia is described as a large and ailing country rich in natural resources, mostly in gas and oil, but incapable of managing them on her own, and therefore, Russia needs foreign advisors.

I was shocked when I discovered that a very nice and perky young journalist from a glossy magazine, who came to interview me in my first month as Ambassador, had never heard about Yuri Gagarin. And then it got me thinking how many graduates of Russian schools would know today that the Soviet Union was a trailblazer in space exploration.

I often gave talks on South Korean TV, radio, in different universities in Seoul and in the provinces. In the beginning of every talk in a university, I would ask what language I should speak. People would normally ask me to speak English since political science is taught in English, and all students are fluent. Judging by the questions asked after such talks, I could see it was, to put it mildly, not quite the case. They asked me about things I had already explained in detail. So I started bringing my own interpreters. Things went on much better. The audience had some questions in the course of the talk, and I could often see what a distorted picture of Russia they had, created for them by Russia's ill-wishers, and I did my best to put things right.

In Korea with its Confucian traditions it is impolite to ask "awkward" questions to a person senior to you either in age or in social status. An ambassador giving a talk in a university is undoubtedly just such a senior person. So no one asked me such "awkward," or, as we used to say in the Soviet times, "provocative" questions. The audience just made sure of some facts.

This is one story that happened to me when I was giving a talk to the students of South Korea's National Defense College. This college is attached to South Korea's Ministry of Defense, offering officer corps refresher training. Its students include military officers having ranks from colonel to brigadier general, and civil officials in equally high positions. Every year in March, they invited me to give a talk on Russia and Russian-Korean relations to their new students. And that year, in early September 2008, after the events in South Ossetia, they asked me to give an extra talk, preferably on the Embassy's premises. They told me they had some problem assigning a college hall for the lecture.

I agreed. Chairs were set up in the Embassy's reception hall, the Koreans bussed in about 80 people, including even one Australian and one Malaysian. I spoke to them in English, the Embassy's interpreter interpreted into Korean. The audience were writing something down. They asked some clarification questions. All in all, a typical talk. Suddenly, a savvy-looking colonel wearing glasses stands up and politely asks, "Mister Ambassador, could you tell us why Georgia and Ukraine were reduced to the status of semi-colonies in the Soviet Union?" I reply, "That would be impossible, since for thirty years, the Soviet Union's leader was a Georgian, and then for thirty more years, the country's leaders were Ukraine-born." The audience are visibly confused. They ask me whom I mean. I ask them, "Do you know Stalin, Khrushchev, and Brezhnev?" Everybody nods assent. "Well," I say, "Stalin was born in Georgia, and Khrushchev and Brezhnev were born in Ukraine. Judge for yourself whether any of them could reduce their homelands to semi-colonies." The consensus was it was impossible. They apologized for not knowing the facts.

South Korea's Interests in Russia

The Republic of Korea's leadership has repeatedly emphasized its interest in developing a strategic Cooperative Partnership with Russia. In this regard, it is worth noting that the present development of the Russia-ROK relationship does not correspond with these high expectations. Both sides are still to do a lot to achieve that level of interaction

South Korea's interest in Russia has a political and economic basis. As for politics, Seoul gives primary importance to cooperation with Russia in ensuring stability and security in Northeast Asia. Firstly, the objective is to deprive Pyongyang of any support from Moscow. Secondly, Russia is needed by South Korea in the region as a sort of a counterbalance to China and Japan. No interaction though, let alone partnership, has been observed in the approaches to key international issues in other regions. Seoul is distancing itself from Moscow in that respect gradually but plainly, following the U.S. line during discussions in the UN and at other international forums.

Economically, Russia is highly attractive for South Korea, which is nearly void of mineral and other natural resources, and thus willing to participate in the development thereof in Siberia and Russia's Far East. Alongside with that, Russia is a promising market for South Korean industrial products.

The South Koreans are willing to cooperate with Russia where Russian technologies still retain high international standards, particularly in space and nuclear energy. Evidence to that is the contract of the Russian Space Agency on the construction of the Naro Space Center of the Republic of Korea; the joint space flight of the first South Korean astronaut Yi So-yeon in April 2008 on board of the Russian spaceship Soyuz TMA-12, with two Russian cosmonauts; the launch of the Russia-ROK Space carrier vehicle

(KSLV-1) in January 2013 which was the first Republic of Korea launch vehicle to achieve Earth orbit; and South Korean import of Russian nuclear power plant fuel, helicopters and certain weaponry and combat systems.

3

South Korea on the Economic Map of the World

Achievements

Today, South Korea is a highly developed country with a significant potential. With a population of 50 million people (0.7 per cent of the global population) it produces about 2 per cent of the world's gross product and has the eighth-largest foreign trade volume. Industry plays an important role in South Korea's economy. The country is the world's leading shipbuilder (40 per cent of the global order portfolio). It's the leading manufacturer of semiconductors and monitors (Samsung Electronics and Hynix, Korea's two leading companies, have cornered more than 50 per cent of the world's semiconductor market), the second-largest maker of cell phones, fifth-largest car manufacturer, and sixth-largest in steel production. Both in the Asian-Pacific and global markets, the Republic of Korea is an important supplier of weapons, including surface-to-air missile systems, armored personnel carriers, infantry fighting vehicles, tanks, planes, warships.

It should be noted that South Korea has a well-developed nuclear power generation industry. Currently, nuclear power plants supply up to 31.5 per cent of the country's energy demand. In addition to the 21 operational nuclear reactors, South Korea plans to build 9 more by the year 2021, and then to construct 8 to 10 more. By the year 2030, nuclear power plants are expected to supply 59 per cent of the country's energy demand. South Korea becomes more and more active in the nuclear power plant export market. In the late 2009, Korea Electric Power Corporation beat European and Japanese companies and won the bid to build a nuclear power plant in the UAE. The contract is worth 40 billion dollars. By the year 2030, South Korea aims to build 80 nuclear power plants across the globe, thus becoming one of the top three nuclear power plants builders in the global market. South Korean nuclear power plants have already attracted attention in Finland and Lithuania. India, too, is leaning toward the South Korean reactors, as do in the long-term prospect Poland, Morocco, and the Philippines.

South Korea has its own space program, too, which testifies to their highly developed rocket engineering. Seoul plans to send its first probe to the moon orbit before 2020, and to have its first probe land on the moon in 2025.

South Korea is focused on constantly improving the quality of its products and on developing innovative services. Between 2001 and 2009, the number of hardwire internet connections in South Korea grew from 7.81 million to 16.35 million, and the number of Internet users grew from 24. 38 million to 36.58 million.

South Korea actively invests abroad and also actively attracts foreign investments. In 2012, these investments reached a total of 210 billion dollars. In 1998, South Korea passed the unified Law on Facilitating Foreign Investments, which subsumed all previously passed legislation concerning foreign investments. It significantly facilitated and unified legal procedures for foreign investors and introduced various preferences, including taxation preferences. In particular, those companies which invest in hi-tech industries are granted seven-year exemption from corporate and income taxes. The state's real estate can be leased for the term of up to fifty years at reduced rates and sometimes even entirely free of charge. Free economic zones for foreign investors have been created, too.

Apart from such traditional spheres as finances and insurance, foreign investments are channeled into South Korea's research and development projects, establishing multinational corporations' logistics centers and even headquarters. Foreign investors' interest in such projects is clear. South Korea's investments into research and development place the country among the top ten in the world, and in the number of patents, it is the fourth in the world after the US, Japan, and China. As far as the prospects of investing into logistics and companies' headquarters, investors proceed on the assumption that Seoul is four hours by plane away from 51 cities with a million of residents each. Not surprisingly, more than a half of the companies on Fortune 500 have an established presence in South Korea.

Problems to be Solved

By the early 1990s, South Korean business encountered a serious problem. During the previous decades, South Korean economy had been developing largely because the country had a large, cheap, and disciplined workforce. South Korean workers had been prepared to work for peanuts, and it allowed South Korea to offer its goods on the global market at very low prices. During the entire industrialization period, from the mid-1970s until the late 1980s, average wages in South Korea's industry were 15 per cent of the average salary in Japan and 11 per cent of the average salary in the US.

However, the population's extremely low income and a high saving rate (even in the early 1990s, it was up to 35 per cent of South Korea's gross national income) weren't the only sources of South Korea's impressive industrial breakthrough. The developing industry demanded a greater workforce recruited from peasants and craftsmen. Industry's share in the GDP grew, and also grew the share of industrial sector's employees. Since the early 1960s and until the early 1990s, it grew from 22 to 48 per cent. At the same time, the share of employed women grew as well, as did the number of daily working hours. As a result, in the early 1990s, South Korea's industrial employees worked nearly 2.5 thousand hours a year, although in the majority of European countries, the number of working hours was legally limited to 1.5 thousand hours.

By the 1990s, South Korea had exhausted its workforce reserves, and wages in South Korea began to grow. Under these new circumstances, South Korean businesses found it much harder to compete with the countries of South and Southeast Asia where the workers were still prepared to work 12 hours a day for a bowl of rice. South Korea had two ways out: either to develop its hi-tech industry and to move into high-end markets, or to move its manufacturing abroad, to the countries with cheap labor. Most companies took both ways.

Among the countries with cheap labor, China and Vietnam were the foremost to attract South Korea's attention. In China, 40,000 South Korean companies invested about 100 billion dollars into China's economy. In Vietnam, South Korea's presence is not so pronounced, with about 2,500 companies and 23 billion in investments. There is yet another aspect to the relations between South Korea and China and Vietnam: Chinese and Vietnamese workers are employed in South Korean enterprises. Some of them entered South Korea on special work visas, but most of them are illegal. From time to time, the authorities round up and deport illegal workers, but on the whole, the authorities turn a blind eye to them. Seoul understands that South Korean industry needs migrant workers from China, Vietnam, the Philippines, Thailand, Sri Lanka, Bangladesh, Mongolia, Central Asia, even sometimes from the Russian Far East. Migrants do those jobs which South Koreans don't want.

South Korea's economy is highly dependent on the situation in the global market (its foreign trade quota is nearly 100 per cent), and the recent global crisis had an extremely negative influence on the country. Its economic development slowed down significantly: in 2012, its GDP growth was only 2.5 per cent, while during the 1990s, it averaged 6 per cent. The industrial manufacturing exhibited a particularly shocking slack, the growth there is below 2 per cent compared to 10-12 per cent it had demonstrated. 3.9 million people in South Korea are unemployed, a number that grew compared to 3.5 million in 2007-2008 when the crisis hit.

The GDP is expected to grow at a slack pace up until the year 2030. One of the principal factors holding that growth back is unfavorable demographic trends.

South Korean population is aging rapidly. In 2014, 10 per cent of the population will be over 65. The prospect of the workforce shrinking is becoming more and more threatening, especially since the majority of the population exhibits a highly negative attitude to employing foreign workers. The workers' average age is growing, and it will have negative consequences for labor efficiency and product quality. Theoretically, South Korea can solve its demographic problem by uniting the two Korean states, as North Korea's population is estimated to be 24 million people. South Korea's long-term prospects offer several more challenges, the principal one being the decreasing competitive edge of Korean products due to their higher costs compared to Chinese products.

Sociopolitical situation is growing worse, and South Korea's society is becoming more and more polarized. After being pushed into the background during the liberal presidencies of Kim Dae-jung and Roh Moo-hyun, right-wing conservatives have consolidated. The younger and better educated part of South Korea's society is thus far disorganized, it doesn't have a charismatic leader, and it can offer no more than passive resistance to the right wing, but it is quite possible that in the nearest future, given the worsening domestic economy, they will put forward an organization and its leaders. As in neighboring China and Japan, South Korea's right-wing and left-wing politicians actively use nationalism as a mobilizing force.

In its foreign policy, South Korea generally follows the US and doesn't propose any far reaching initiatives. At the same time, as it pumps up its economic muscles, South Korea is pushing for certain autonomy, and attempts to stick to its guns in the issues of economic and trading cooperation and research and development cooperation aimed at solidifying its positions in the markets for natural resources and engineering products.

It's a telltale fact that South Korea presents its economic breakthrough as a model to be imitated, particularly by the developing countries of the "third world." This trend was especially obvious when South Korea was pushing for Ban Ki-moon's candidacy for the UN's Secretary General. Today, South Korean companies are very active in the developing world: in Southeast Asia, in the Persian Gulf, in Africa, and in South America.

At the same time, South Korea's agenda includes joining

Northeast Asia's three-party economic bloc together with China and Japan. The combined population of the three countries is about 1.5 billion people (22 per cent of the global population), their combined GDP is over 10 trillion dollars (1/5 of the global GDP), and their combined three-party trade volume is about 7.6 trillion dollars (over 16 per cent of the overall global trading). The new regional group could be the third largest in the world after NAFTA and the EU. The economic conditions for this bloc have long been in place. In 2012, the Chinese-South Korean trade volume was 220 billion dollars, and Japanese-South Korean trade volume was 11o billion dollars. Up to 30 per cent of South Korea's trade is done with China and Japan. South Koreans expect this free trade agreement to guarantee the growth of their GDP by 1.46 per cent for ten years. Should this agreement be signed, it will form a unified market of 14.3 trillion dollars. It would be South Korea's third largest free trade agreement after similar agreements with the US and the EU. At the same time, South Korea is preparing an economic partnership agreement with the countries of Southeast Asia. That agreement is analogous to the free trade agreement, and it implies participation of the ten ASEAN countries and their six free trade partners: the Republic of Korea, the People's Republic of China, Japan, Australia, New Zealand, and India.

For South Koreans, their cooperation with India is of growing importance. In 2009, the two countries signed a free trade agreement which India proposed calling Comprehensive Economic Partnership Agreement. It covers, first and foremost, IT, engineering, and finances. Bilateral trade volume reached 20.5 billion dollars in 2011, and in 2015, it should increase to over 40 billion dollars. Mutual investments are growing, too; South Korea invested 5 billion dollars in India, and India invested over 1 billion dollars in South Korea. Leading South Korean companies working in India include Hyundai Motors, Samsung Electronics,

LG Electronics, Lotte Group, and Doosan Heavy Industries. South Korea's POSCO, one of the world's leading steel-making companies, intends to build a steel works with the capacity of 12 million tons of steel per year.

4

Legacy of the Korean War

The War With No Winners

Today's Republic of Korea is a prosperous and successful state, but it has one festering wound, the legacy of the Korean War. This subject inevitably comes up in every conversation with South Koreans. July 27, 2013 marked the sixtieth anniversary of the Korean Armistice Agreement which put an end to the three-year war, the bloodiest and the most destructive military conflict after World War II. The consequences of the Korean War still hold their sway over the international situation in Northeast Asia and beyond.

The principal trends which determined the global development in the mid-20th century were also reflected in the events in Korea and around it. The Soviet Army played the leading role in defeating the Nazi Germany and the militaristic Japan in World War II, and consequently, the West no longer played the leading role in the global affairs. That caused the West's resentment, and the Cold War started. The Soviet victory was augmented with the victory of the Communist China, the colonial empires began to crumble, with India and other decolonized states all over the world and particularly in Asia building their independent statehood.

Between 1910 and 1945, Korea was Japan's colony. In accordance with the agreement between the Allies, the USSR, the US, and the UK, Korea had to become independent of the defeated Japan. The country was divided at the 38th parallel. To the north of the line, the Japanese troops surrendered to the Soviet Army, to the south, they surrendered to the US army.

In December 1945, a conference of Ministers of Foreign Affairs of the USSR, the US, and the UK was convened in Moscow, and the decision was reached concerning Korea's provisional trusteeship, and a Soviet-US joint commission was formed with the view to establishing Korea's provisional democratic government; the committee was supposed to put forward proposal developed after consultations with Korean democratic parties and public organizations. While the Soviet Union relied on the left wing forces which were on the rise after the Korean liberation from the colonial yoke, the US relied on the right-wing forces. The committee deadlocked, and in September 1947, the US submitted the Korean issue to the UN. By the 1949, Soviet and American armed forces had been withdrawn from the Korean territory.

In May 1948, separate UN-supervised elections were held in South Korea. On August 15, 1948, the Republic of Korea was established, and elderly professor Syng Man Rhee who had lived in the US for over thirty years, became the Republic's President. The government of South Korea claimed that it had jurisdiction over all of Korea. Naturally, the Communists in the North did not agree. In the summer of 1948, they held elections for the Supreme People's Assembly, and on September 9, 1948, the Assembly proclaimed the Democratic People's Republic of Korea

(DPRK) headed by Kim Il-sung, the leader of Korean communists, who arrived in Korea from the USSR in 1945.

Opinions differ as to who struck the first spark to inflame the blazes of the Korean War. Anton Chekhov had once written that if there is a gun on the wall in the first act of the play, then the gun should fire at the third act of the play. And by June 1950, Korea had accumulated enough guns both north and south of the 38th parallel.

The Korean War which started on June 25, 1950 was in its essence a civil war between two Korean camps, one of the North which intended to follow the Soviet model, and the other of the South which proclaimed its commitment to the American way. But it was the time of the Cold War, and the local conflict grew into a large-scale military engagement which nearly peaked in a nuclear strike. Directly or indirectly the war involved the powerful countries: the US, the UK, the USSR, the PRC, and also the UN which sent to Korea a multinational military force under its flag to support the South.

The war laid waste to Korea. Some historians claim that the US bombed Korea more intensely than it did Germany and Japan during World War II. The war took millions of Korean lives. Several hundred thousands of Chinese volunteers, tens of thousands of Americans and soldiers from many other countries fighting in the UN troops also lost their lives in the Korean War.

There were no winners in the Korean War. Neither North, nor South achieved their objectives. The War was stopped right where it had been started. Korea was left divided at the same 38th parallel with the Democratic People's Republic of Korea in the north, and the Republic of Korea in the south. Korea's division was confirmed by the two opposed global forces. In accordance with the Cold War standards, the USSR, the PRC, and other socialist countries ignored the Republic of Korea, while the US and its allies did not recognize the DPRK.

Today, just like sixty years ago, the demilitarized zone which separates the two states is surrounded on both sides with troops many thousands strong, armed with state-of-the-art weapons. And those troops aren't Korean only. Although Chinese volunteers were withdrawn from the DPRK back in 1958, the US still has up to thirty thousand troops in South Korea in accordance with the US-South Korea Mutual Defense Treaty. This U.S - Korea Combined Forces Command is under an American general who, in case of a military conflict on the Korean Peninsula, will command the Republic of Korea's Armed Forces as well.

De jure, the two Korean states are still at war since the Armistice Agreement signed on July 27, 1953 is nothing more than the Commanders-in-Chief agreeing on a temporary truce. The agreement was signed by Marshal Kim Il-sung, Commander-in-Chief of the Korean People's Army, representing North Korea; by General Peng Dehuai, commander of the Chinese people's volunteers; and by American General Mark W. Clark, Commander-in-Chief of the United Nations Command. There is no signature of a South Korean military officer since South Korean army was commanded by General Clark. The Armistice Agreement is still the only guarantee of peace and stability in the peninsula; this Agreement determines the demilitarized zone (DMZ) regime of the border than runs between North and South along the 38th parallel.

As far as the UN is concerned, it removed the issue of Korean political settlement from its agenda in November 1975, after simultaneously passing two contradictory resolutions, one supported by 28 countries including the US, and the other supported by 43 countries including the USSR. The UN returned to the Korean issue only in 1991 when UN membership was granted to both the DPRK and the ROK.

The Korean War and Its International Consequences

The US used the Korean situation to increase its military presence in Asia. Demanding to stop "the spread of Communism," the US aimed to form US-led military alliances in Asia Pacific in addition to NATO established in Europe in 1949.

What is particularly telling is the US about-face in its relations with Japan, its recent enemy in World War II. Already in 1951, the US signed a security treaty with Japan granting the US the right to station military bases in the Japanese territory with an unlimited number of troops. In 1951, the ANZUS bloc treaty was signed (Australia - New Zealand - USA Pacific Security Treaty). In the fall of 1953, the US and South Korea signed the Mutual Defense Treaty. In 1954, the Southeast Asia Collective Defense Treaty (SEATO), or the Manila Pact was signed. In the same year, the US concluded a mutual security pact with Taiwan and stationed 10,000 troops on the island.

At the same time, the Korean Armistice had already demonstrated the inability of the US to resolve important international issues by force, to impose its stance on the international community. The Korean War convinced both the international community and the USSR and the US of the dangers of military conflicts escalating to a potential nuclear attack. The Korean War led to the global upsurge of antiwar, anti-bloc, and, in Asia and Africa, anti-imperialistic sentiments.

As far as Moscow was concerned, the 20th Congress of the Communist Party of the Soviet Union held in February 1956 set down the tenets of the peaceful co-existence of the two systems and of war prevention. The influence of both the USSR and China among the third-world countries significantly increased;

there was their rapprochement with India which had taken great efforts in the UN to stop the war in Korea and also a rapprochement with Indonesia, Egypt, and other countries which originated the Non-Aligned Movement.

Two Koreas: A Long Way Apart

For many years, the two Korean states moved along parallel tracks. The DPRK relied on the Soviet and Chinese support. In 1961, North Korea signed the North Korean-Soviet Mutual Aid and Cooperation Friendship Treaty and the Sino-North Korean Mutual Aid and Cooperation Friendship Treaty. Both treaties provided for military aid in case of a military aggression against one of the parties. The Republic of Korea, in its turn, based its politics and policies on its alliance with the US, confirmed by the Mutual Defense Treaty signed in September 1953.

Both Pyongyang and Seoul wished to unite the country, each on its own terms, and each strove to gain advantage over its rival. By the late 1960s, the DPRK's economy developed much quicker than that of South Korea. The situation changed in the 1970s, when South Korea seized the lead due to President Park Chung-hee's reforms. By the late 1970s, Seoul had established diplomatic relations with over 100 states, Pyongyang, with over 70 states. Both Koreas were members of various international organizations and were Permanent Observers to the UN.

From time to time, both Pyongyang and Seoul put forward their proposals for Korea's unification. However, these proposals were meant for purely domestic consumption. The state of inter-Korean relations was determined by the state of relations between the East and the West, between the USSR, the US, and China. Not accidentally, the first joint North-South declaration to the effect that Korea's unification should be achieved by Koreans themselves, without any foreign interference, as a result of a peaceful process based on "national consolidation," was made on July 4, 1972. The declaration was preceded by US President Richard Nixon's visit to Beijing in February 1972, which improved the American-Chinese relations, and by Soviet-American summit in Moscow in May 1972, which inaugurated the period of detente between the US and the USSR.

The end of the Cold War had its effect on the Korean Peninsula, too. Moscow made its move and established diplomatic relations with the Republic of Korea in 1990. It would have been natural to expect an adequate response from the West, especially since both Koreas were granted UN membership in 1991, and China followed the Soviet example and opened its embassy in Seoul in 1992. However, neither the US nor its allies recognized the DPRK; it appeared that Gorbachev never bothered to agree on "cross-recognition" for both Koreas, and when Yeltsin came to power, he put all his eggs in the South Korean basket.

Under these circumstances, Koreans themselves got down to establishing the inter-Korean dialog. In December 1991, heads of government of North and South Koreas recognized formally the equality of the two Korean states and signed the Agreement on Reconciliation, Non-aggression, Exchanges and Cooperation and the Joint Declaration on the Denuclearization of the Korean Peninsula. Two contributing factors were the collapse of the military dictatorship in South Korea which was now led by a democratically elected government, and the loss of economic and political support North Korea used to receive from the USSR and the Warsaw Pact countries.

For Pyongyang, it was no longer the question of pitting its strength against Seoul, it was now the question of survival. North Korean leaders shifted the emphasis from Marxism and socialism onto national traditions and Confucian values and proclaimed the policy of Seon'gun as the country's survival strategy. The policy gave the army top priority, and included heavy military preparations and developing North Korea's own nuclear program. As a result, in the mid-1990s, the country was starving, yet total isolation from the outside world, its unity in the face of possible aggression by the US and its allies, the citizens' habit of taking any difficulties and privations as natural allowed Pyongyang to overcome all trials.

The resilience of the North prompted Kim Dae-jung, South Korea's first liberal president, to propose the "sunshine policy" which included holding the first ever North Korea-South Korea summit in June 2000. Kim Dae-jung's visit to Pyongyang and his meetings with North Korea's leader Kim Jong-il resulted in the Joint Declaration, a kind of a road map for developing bilateral relations, aimed at gradually turning away from confrontation and at reconciliation and gradual rapprochement. President Roh Moo-hyun continued Kim Dae-jung's policy, and the second North-South summit in 2007 was another step toward rapprochement between of the two countries.

Relations with North Korea: A Wide Range of Approaches

When I arrived in Seoul in 2005, I discovered the wide range of approaches South Koreans had to their relations with North Korea. On the one hand, South Korea still had the Law on National Security, which predated the Korean War. Under this law, the DPRK is "a territory controlled by an anti-state organization," and consequently, all unsanctioned contacts between South Koreans and North Koreans, trips to the North, and publicly expressed pro-Pyongyang sentiments are to be considered "aiding the enemy" and national security violations, which formally carry severe penalty up to and including the death penalty.

On the other hand, conversations on the subject of inter-Korean relations with intellectuals of the older generation, with university professors, for instance, were somehow reminiscent of Russian liberals' discussions from the time of Gorbachev's perestroika, although with opposite assessments. Any positive attitude to Park Chung-hee's contribution to the "Korean economic miracle" was treated like praising Stalin would have been in 1989 Moscow: "How can you say good things about him? He's a murderous dictator, his hands are covered in blood of thousands of people!" And the name of Kim Il-sung produced a somewhat benevolent reaction: "Yes, he wasn't a democrat, but he sincerely strove to preserve the country's unity." As far as the young generation is concerned, they are equally far removed from Park Chung-hee, and from Kim Il-sung and Kim Jong-il. South Korean youth, permeated with consumerist and hedonistic spirit, views North Korea not as a part that was cut off from their united homeland, but just a neighboring state, even if not the most friendly one, whose population also speaks Korean. Well, then, the population of Canada and the US also speak the same language, as do people in Argentine and Uruguay. At the same time, it was hard to ignore violent street fighting going on for over a week around the monument to General MacArthur who commanded American troops during the Korean War. The fighting took place in the fall of 2005 in Incheon, South Korea's third-largest city. Left-wing students demanded that the monument to MacArthur be dismantled since the general had been responsible for the split of Korea. They were opposed and finally overcome by the still tough South Korean veterans of the Korean War who were grateful to MacArthur for "saving Korea from communism."

Members of Roh Moo-hyun's liberal administration, in particular, Chung Dong-young, the charismatic Minister of Unification, who had come into politics after working on television, claimed that the way to unification lay through economic integration. He quoted the example of Kaesong Industrial Region, built in North Korea, close to the demilitarized zone, with South Korean money. The minister expected the example of Kaesong Industrial Region which united two economic systems, to gradually, on the span of about twenty years, spread around the entire DPRK, thus creating economic foundations for the political unification of the two countries.

Inter-Korean Dialog

Both Kim Dae-jung's "sunshine policy" and Roh Moo-hyun's "policy of peace and prosperity" were aimed at proceeding toward unification via economic integration of North and South Koreas. Pyongyang saw cooperation with the South as the means to enliven its economy given its limited sources of outside help. Since 2003, South Korea was the DPRK's second-largest trading partner after China.

Kaesong Industrial Region located in the DPRK close to the South Korean border, is thus far the largest and most successful inter-Korean project. More than a hundred small and medium South Korean businesses opened their production facilities in that region. North Korea provided cheap labor. In 2012, due to Kaesong Industrial Region, inter-Korean trade volume approached 2 billion dollars. Regular railway service through the demilitarized zone was opened in 2007. Kaesong Industrial Region which united two economic systems became an example of practical economic integration of North and South. The agreements achieved at the second inter-Korean summit of 2007 stipulated creating similar industrial regions in other North Korean districts.

When in 2008, liberal Roh Moo-hyun stepped down and conservative Lee Myong-bak assumed presidency, when tension grew due to North Korea's nuclear program, inter-Korean relations suffered a serious setback. All connections between North and South Koreas, including meetings between Ministers, economic negotiations, and defense contacts, were cut.

Inter-Korean relations were gravely challenged in 2010. In March, South Korean corvette *Cheonan* sank in the Yellow Sea killing nearly half of its crew. South Korea's President Lee Myong-bak held North Korea responsible. In November 2010, the relations suffered another setback after North Korean artillery fired at a South Korean island in the Yellow Sea, on the border between the two countries.

The Nuclear Issue of the Korean Peninsula

It is quite clear why Pyongyang started its own nuclear program. When the Cold War ended, the US undertook a series of unilateral aggressions against those states which somehow displeased the US, and the international community represented by the UN turned out to be powerless to oppose it. Washington knew Yugoslavia had no weapons of mass destruction, and together with their NATO allies, the US coldheartedly bombed and dismembered this once influential state. The US expended significant efforts to have the UN experts confirm that Iraq had no weapons of mass destruction, and then occupied Iraq. Naturally, under those circumstances, none of those states Washington branded as "rogue" states would never voluntarily give up on any means of guaranteeing their security, no matter how radical those means might be. The events in Libya serve as the most recent argument in support of this stance. The Libyan leader Gaddafi voluntarily gave up on developing nuclear weapons, and the world saw the kind of appreciation the West showed him. So Pyongyang's policies are quite understandable, especially since in the 1970s, South Korea also tried to develop its own nuclear program.

North Korean leaders have always been and certainly still are aware of the fact that for them, to start any war, especially a nuclear war, would be suicidal. Therefore North-Korean nuclear preparations are determined by other reasons besides the purely military ones. The propaganda campaign surrounding North Korean nuclear program is an effective means of mobilizing the North Korean society, uniting it around the country's leaders who "fight back the aggressive machinations of American imperialists and their South Korean puppets." At the same time, North Korean leaders hope to use negotiating the curtailment of their nuclear program as a lever to obtain economic aid and investments from those same Americans and South Koreans.

That plan already worked in the 1990s. During Bill Clinton's presidency, the US practiced an "appeasement policy" in its relations with North Korea. In 1994, former president Jim Carter visited Pyongyang and met with Kim Il-sung, and subsequently in Geneva, the two countries signed the Agreed Framework between the United States of America and the Democratic People's Republic of Korea aimed at settling the Korean Peninsula nuclear crisis. North Korea agreed to freeze its nuclear program, and in exchange, North Korea was supposed to have two light water reactors built, it was promised shipments of American oil for North Korean thermal power plants, and also the improved political relations between Pyongyang and Washington, including mutual recognition. The Korean Peninsula Energy Development Organization (KEDO), an international body comprising the US, South Korea, Japan, and the European Union, was formed in 1995 to build nuclear power plants in North Korea. South Korea and Japan provided most of the financial backing. In 2000, the world media widely publicized photos of Kim Jong-il together with the-then US State Secretary M. Albright. Her visit to

Pyongyang was believed to be a preparation for the-then President Bill Clinton's visit to North Korea.[1]

The arrival of George W. Bush's Republican administration sharply changed the US stance. All negotiations with Pyongyang were stopped. The US President included North Korea into the so-called "axis of evil" which, Washington claimed, threatened peace and stability in the world. Simultaneously, North Korea also took a more hard-line position, withdrew from the Treaty on the Non-Proliferation of Nuclear Weapons and conducted its first nuclear test in 2006.

The test made no particular splash in Seoul. Newspapers and TV made some noise, but the government declared it would no longer provide humanitarian aid to Pyongyang, placed its armed forces on limited alert which had been done many times in the past for a variety of different reasons, and stopped at that. Economic cooperation, bilateral trade went on uninterrupted, and Kaesong Industrial Region also did business as usual. I remember a television crew from the Moscow NTV channel team urgently dispatched to Seoul in search of sensations. I had to grievously disappoint them, as there were no blackouts in Seoul, there was the usual heavy traffic in Seoul streets, and everyone continued with their life and work as usual.

I have no doubts that some South Koreans even rejoiced in secret when North Korea conducted its test. I personally heard words to the effect that if North Koreans really had conducted a nuclear test, all Koreans should be proud of Korean brains and hands constructing such a weapon, and when Korea is united, it will take its rightful place among nuclear powers.

---

1. It should be noted that M. Albright visited Pyongyang in October 2000, after the new Treaty on Friendship, Good Neighborly Relations, and Cooperation between the Russian Federation and the DPRK was concluded on February 9, 2000, and after Vladimir Putin visited Pyongyang on July 19-20, 2000.

The nuclear issue of the Korean Peninsula has direct bearing on Russia. North Korea conducts its tests no more than 150-300 kilometers from the Russian border. That is not something we are happy about. We don't need either nuclear, or missile tests conducted close to our borders. We don't need any saber-rattling from anybody.

It should also be taken into account that North Korea's example could push other "threshold" or "pre-threshold" states to develop their own nuclear weapons. Even now some forces in Japan, South Korea, and Taiwan call upon their governments to develop their own nuclear weapons. Nuclear technologies and nuclear weapons components developed by Pyongyang should be guaranteed to never fall into the hands of troubled countries or organizations.

In 2003, Russia, China, North Korea, South Korea, the US and Japan started six-party talks on the nuclear issue of the Korean peninsula. Their joint statement of September 19, 2005 laid the foundations for moving both toward Korean Peninsula's denuclearization and to the general improvement of the situation in the region. Putting those resolutions into practice would achieve the economic and political decisions that would make Northeast Asia a region of peace, security, and cooperation.

What did this statement contain specifically? North Korea's statement that it was ready to abandon its nuclear weapons and all its nuclear programs, and, within a short time, to re-join the Non-proliferation Treaty and the IAEA regime. The US's statement that it had no nuclear weapons in the Korean Peninsula, had no intention to invade North Korea or attack its territory with nuclear or conventional weapons. The statement that both the US and the DPRK were ready to officially respect each other's sovereignty, to exist peacefully together, and to take steps to improve their bilateral relations. The statement concerning the six parties' commitment to peace and stability in Northeast Asia. A statement concerning the parties' agreement to develop a compromise formula which would allow the DPRK's future peaceful nuclear programs, including building a light water reactor. The adoption of the consensus principle for implementing the agreements achieved: "commitment for commitment, action for action." The parties agreed to form five working groups: on the denuclearization of the Korean Peninsula, normalization of North Korea-U.S. relations, normalization of North Korea-Japan relations, economy and energy cooperation, as well as a joint Northeast Asia peace and security mechanism. Russia was put in charge of the Working Group for the joint Northeast Asia peace and security mechanism which is a far greater issue than the denuclearization of the Korean Peninsula.

The parties agreed to hold another meeting at the ministerial level, which would confirm the Joint Statement of September 19, 2005 and lay the groundwork for developing cooperation in North Asia security. The parties also agreed to hold a special forum to discuss a stable peace regime in the Korean Peninsula.

However, these achievements are now up in the air. Not all parties were able to implement them. Why? Because some parties, and the US in particular, are interested in Northeast Asia remaining a hotbed of tension.

The Prospects of Korean Unification and the Possible Changes in the North

The nuclear issue of the Korean Peninsula is the direct consequence of confrontation between the two Korean states. And its settlement is closely linked to the normalization of inter-Korean relations, with the movement toward Korea's reunification. These are the two wheels of the same cart which could take the region's states to their common destination which is peace and security in Northeast Asia.

Korea and Germany are often compared as two states whose people were divided after World War II. Reunification of Germany in 1990 spurred hopes for Korea's future unification. At the same time it is clear that neither Pyongyang nor Seoul is ready for unification. North Koreans are said to be scared by Germany's example where the capitalist West is alleged to have rudely trampled upon the socialist East with the East Germans having been made "second rate citizens." The South is alleged to be afraid of prohibitive costs of bringing North Korea's economy and society on par with those of South Korea. The National Assembly of South Korea commissioned a calculation of the costs which were estimated to be between 850 billion and 1.3 trillion dollars.

These arguments do have some truth to them, but the key difference between Korea and Germany should be noted. East Germans had never been at war with West Germans, while the Korean War of 1950-1953 started as a civil war which eventually drew in foreign participants. The memory of the hundreds of thousands who died in that war, the memory of Koreans killed by Koreans, is still alive. The war led to a clear political and geographical demarcation of Korea: people with left-wing views went to the North, people with right-wing views went to the South.

Seoul has always viewed, and still does view the unification of Korea as South Korea subsuming North Korea. Both Lee Myong-bak's confrontational policies, and Kim Dae-jong's and Roh Moo-hyun's "sunshine policy" were two sides of the same coin. Currently, South Korea is enhancing its military potential, which would allow it to play a more important role in the region. The ROK boasts a sizable military might. As for its strength, the

South Korean armed forces were ranked in the top 10 of the world until recently. It is with far-reaching goals that South Korea acquires new military technology: it is suitable for safeguarding military interests of a united Korea. These acquisitions include the *Sejong the Great* class destroyers of 7,600 tons displacement, featuring Aegis combat system; type 214 submarines and Hyunmoo-3 long-range cruise missile with a range of 1,500 kilometers.

Lee Myong-bak, former president of South Korea, proclaimed "global Korea" to be one of the goals of his foreign policy. South Korea's Ministry of Defense stated it would develop a multifaceted military diplomacy in order to turn South Korea into an "established world nation." South Koreans, however, are scared by the price tag: even if unification goes peacefully, the expenses involved in improving North Korea's economy would for a long time push the united Korea right out of the global market competition.

For Pyongyang, it is not only the matter of their ideological confrontation with the South, or of their fears that unification might result in the restitution of property to its former Southern owners. North Korea initiated its own changes. Thus far, these changes are very moderate, they can always be stopped or pushed back, but Kim Jong-il started the process, and Kim Jong-un appears to give an additional impetus to those changes. North Korea's development appears obvious: the country is transitioning toward a market economy based on the Chinese or the similar Vietnamese model. However, North Korea has its own specifics, which means direct Chinese-style reforms would be extremely dangerous. When in 1978, Deng Xiaoping-led pragmatists in the Communist party of China started their reforms, an average Chinese had nowhere to look to see the practical implementation of the market economy and its results for Americans, the English, the Japanese, or for the Chinese themselves. Taiwan and Hong

Kong were overseas and inaccessible for the mainland Chinese. The citizens of the People's Republic of China had no way to see the life there, people's level of income, and had only official Chinese media's reports, fully monitored and controlled by the Communist Party of China, to assess the situation in those regions.

North Korea's situation is entirely different. The democratic South Korea which is far more rich and free is close by, just across the demilitarized zone, a little bit over 200 kilometers away from Pyongyang. That is why should North Korean reforms ever materialize, they will be very different from the Chinese ones.

North Korean reformers should be far more careful about their reforms than the Chinese reformers. The Damocles sword of South Korea's proximity will force North Korea's reformers to tighten ideological screws and postpone political liberalization. This is the difference between North Korea and China which has radically liberalized its political regime over the last 20-30 years. Yet even in Seoul, the first three decades of the "Korean economic miracle" were marked by a harsh authoritarianism.

However, the success of North Korea's market reforms largely hinges on the success Pyongyang's reformers will have in striking an alliance with North Korea's emerging bourgeoisie which has become significantly entrenched in the country over the last decade.

Pyongyang's opponents count on North Korea's burgeoning entrepreneurs to form an opposition to the regime at some point. This development cannot be altogether discarded. Yet it is not particularly likely that the new North Korean bourgeoisie will act as the "fifth column" in the North-South confrontation and will promote Seoul's interests. The fact of the matter is that the burgeoning North Korean entrepreneurs, regardless of their business, are interested in preserving North Korea's independent statehood. Neither North Korea's finances, nor its technologies would be able to compete against South Korean companies should they be granted access to the North Korean market.

Therefore, in order to succeed in their reforms, North Korean leaders need more than a mere dialog, they need an active alliance with the new bourgeoisie. In China, Deng Xiaoping and other high-ranking party officials largely created the Chinese bourgeoisie from scratch, oftentimes transforming the younger generation of the party elite into this new bourgeois class. Similar developments took place in the 1990s in Myanmar which had no national bourgeoisie (in the old Burma, people engaged in business were Indians or the Chinese, not the Burmese themselves). The military leader Ne Win's regime with its "Burmese way to socialism" failed, and the new military regime led by lieutenant colonels and majors who came to power in 1988, started the denationalization of the economy, transforming former field commanders into managers of various private enterprises. North Korea already has its own, fairly influential bourgeoisie, North Korea's private enterprises are thinly disguised as state-owned. All it takes is changing the official labels and acknowledging the real proprietors' right to ownership.

Another issue is procuring the financial means required for reforms. Pyongyang does need the money, but it has virtually no foreign allies. North Korea could place some hopes with China. After all, Beijing did strongly recommend that North Korea undertake market reforms. However, it is also possible that once North Korea's economy improves its efficiency through state-private partnerships, Pyongyang will gradually attract investors from other countries.

Do All Korea's Neighboring States Want it to Unite?

Given the current political alignment along Russia's Far Eastern border, Russia is interested in Korea being a unified, independent, neutral, and non-nuclear state. Russia invariably supports bridging the gaps between Seoul and Pyongyang and the steps the two Korean states take toward an independent and peaceful unification.

The US, though, would be interested not so much in the united Korea, as in retaining the status quo on the Korean Peninsula, maintaining the hotbed of tension there, as it is the easiest way to preserve or, should need be, even enhance, the American military and political presence in Northeast Asia.

The Japanese are afraid of the emergence of a unified Korea as its powerful regional and global competitor, just like Britain and France tried to stall the reunification of Germany twenty five years ago.

China, in its turn, considers the current alignment in the Korean peninsula through the lens of its confrontation with the US. Beijing quite naturally sees the proclaimed American return to Asia and the transformed American-Japanese-South Korean military partnership as a threat of besiegement. Under such circumstances, China is strategically interested in preserving the DPRK.

Both Pyongyang and Beijing used to say that North Korea and China "depend on each other like lips and teeth," that "their friendship has been tempered by blood," as tens of thousands of Chinese people's volunteers had perished in the Korean War fighting for the North.

Attention is often drawn to the 1961 Sino-North Korean Mutual Aid and Cooperation Friendship Treaty. Yet this treaty does not provide for a military alliance. According to the Chinese, that treaty doesn't at all imply that should the US attack North Korea, Beijing would be bound to provide military aid to North Korea up to and including immediate military engagement. And should Beijing decide that, given the current alignment, North Korea's action can lead to a regional conflict, China has the right to protest in accordance with Article I of the Treaty which states that "the Contracting Parties will continue to make every effort to safeguard the peace of Asia and the world and the security of all peoples."

After the establishment of diplomatic relations with Seoul in 1992, Beijing is actively enhancing its relations with South Korea. Today, the two countries claim to be strategic partners, and their mutual trade volume is about 220 billion dollars, which made China South Korea's top foreign trade partner. (The volume of trade between China and North Korea is about 6 billion dollars).

China is not interested in a military conflict with either the US or South Korea. This is why Beijing is fairly restrained and constructive in its stance regarding North Korea and calls upon all parties "to remain level-headed and restrained, not to provoke each other, and not to undertake any actions which could aggravate the current situation." Beijing also expresses hope that "all parties, being mindful of the long-term prospects, to conduct an active dialog and establish contacts to improve relations, alleviate the situation, denuclearize the peninsula and thereby achieve long-term peace."

Russia and "the Korean Issue"

In the six-party talks, and in Asia Pacific in general, Russia conducts its own independent policy. It equally applies to Russia's stance on North Korea. North Korea is a member of the UN and of other international organizations. The international community has largely recognized North Korea. The only countries which haven't thus far recognized the DPRK are South Korea, the US, and Japan.

In the late 1980s-early 1990s, the relations between Moscow

and Pyongyang suffered a decline. Vladimir Putin's visit to North Korea in 2000 and signing of the Treaty on Friendship, Good Neighborly Relations and Cooperation between Russia and the DPRK laid the groundwork for the renewal of full-scale relations between Russia and North Korea. The Treaty lays special emphasis on the speediest unification of Korea on the basis of independence, peaceful unification, and national consolidation, all the principles agreed upon by both North and South Koreas in their Joint Declaration of July 4, 1972. The recently settled issue of North Korea's debt to Russia is meant to provide a powerful impetus for bilateral economic and trading cooperation between Russia and the DPRK.

Russia could contribute to inter-Korean normalization, too, especially should large three-party projects involving Russia and both Korea, such as the Europe-Korea international railway corridor and the Russia-North Korea-South Korea gas pipeline, be implemented.

From the Nuclear Threat to a Peace Treaty Proposal

Another eruption of tension in the Korean Peninsula happened in the spring of 2013. World media kicked up a racket about a new war brewing in Korea about to start World War III. Just as before, everything was blamed on Pyongyang.

But was it only Pyongyang's fault? North Korea threatened crushing blows against its enemies, but it only spoke about retaliatory strikes in case of an attack on North Korea.

Last year, new leaders came to power in both Koreas. New leaders are clearly symbolic: on the eve of the 60th anniversary of the end of the Korean War, leadership in both countries was assumed by direct descendants of those people who for decades had symbolized the confrontation between two Koreas: in North Korea, it was Kim Jong-un, grandson of Kim Il-sung who had been North Korea's leader for many years, and in Seoul, it was Park Geun-hye, daughter of Park Chung-hee, the creator of the "Korean economic miracle," Kim Il-sung's opponent in the 1960s-1970s. It appeared as if certain forces on both sides of the 38th parallel and beyond decided to test both Kim's and Park's ability to continue what had been started by their grandfather and father respectively.

The conflict began to spiral out after December 12, 2012 when DPRK broke the UN Security Council prohibition on its missile tests and launched its first artificial satellite. The UN Security Council condemned this launch and passed another resolution approving sanctions against DPRK. Pyongyang sharply rejected this decision, and in order to show the entire world that it was holding fast to its nuclear policies, it conducted its third nuclear test on February 12, 2013. The UN Security Council condemned that test, too, and in its statement of March 9, North Korea's Ministry of Foreign Affairs particularly emphasized that " 'the sanctions resolution' passed by the US and its allies are aimed at preventing North Korea from space exploration and at weakening its nuclear containment forces, but it will only lead to Seon'gun Korea increasing its power thousandfold."

Subsequently, the US and South Korea held large-scale joint military exercise using American strategic bombers carrying nuclear weapons; bombers flew out of the island of Guam and the state of Missouri. Pyongyang followed up with threats of missile strikes against South Korea and the US, proclaimed its withdrawal from the Armistice Agreement of 1953. Unlike all other inter-Korean incidents, this one led to the work stoppage at Kaesong Industrial Region.

By the end of May 2013, the propaganda dust raised by the Korean confrontation had finally settled. On May 29, Pyongyang suggested to Seoul that the two states sign a peace treaty to replace the Armistice agreement concluded after the Korean War of 1950 - 1953. On June 9, in the village of Panmunjom, the first working meeting of the North and South Korean representatives took place. North Korea also suggested to the US holding a summit to discuss reducing tension in the Korean Peninsula. Washington did not reject the suggestion outright. Kaesong Industrial Region resumed work.

This is generally good news. All the parties concerned should make every effort to proceed toward settling the "Korean issue." Resuming six-party talks and implementing the obligations undertaken on September 19, 2005 could serve as a starting point. Those who believe that complete nuclear disarmament of North Korea should precede settling any political problems left over since the Korean War are wrong. All the issues should be tackled at once, both freezing and then dismantling North Korea's nuclear program with the country's subsequent re-accession to the Non-proliferation agreement with IAEA guarantees, and the political detente in the Korean Peninsula coupled with developing North Korea's relations with South Korea and other countries of the region.

A peace treaty or another diplomatic instrument designed to sooner or later replace the 1953 Korean Armistice Agreement should be not a mere non-aggression pact between the two countries, but a partnership instrument of a far larger scale turning North Korea from a rogue state into a full member of the international community, a recipient of aid from international monetary organizations, etc.

It has been noted, however, that the Korean War would be hard to conclude with a peace treaty typical for states or alliances of states involved in a military conflict. One obstacle is that North Korea's official stance proclaimed in its constitution holds that there is only one legitimate authority on the Korean Peninsula, that of the North Korean government in Pyongyang. South

Korea's situation mirrors the North Korean one. Under South Korea's constitution, the only legitimate government in the Korean Peninsula is the South Korean government in Seoul.

International aspects of the Korean War also have their specifics. Legally speaking, neither the US, nor China took part in the Korean War, although in fact, the troops of those two countries played the decisive role in the military campaign.

In 1953, those circumstances did not block the Armistice Agreement, even though they did cause their share of difficulties. For a variety of political and diplomatic reasons, South Korea's government refused to affix its signature to the Armistice Agreement which was consequently signed by the Americans acting as the UN troops, by the Chinese represented by "Chinese people's volunteers," and by North Korea's representatives who were the only signatories to use their real names.

Signing a peace treaty will require radical emendations of both Koreas' constitutions. In particular, it will require the removal of both Koreas' frequently repeated statement that Korean unification is the principal goal of Seoul's and Pyongyang's diplomacy.

There is nothing inherently impossible about it. After all, the two German states did come up with similar statements in 1972. Both states recognized each other's sovereignty and established diplomatic relations. Yet Korea is not ready for such a step now, and any attempts to proceed along these lines will prompt a speedy and harsh reaction in both South and North Koreas.

As far as the potential parties to this agreement, those, as provided in the joint Korean declaration of July 4, 1972, could be the two Korean states with the US, China, Russia, and Japan acting as guarantors of peace and cooperation between them. These four states are particularly interested in ensuring security in Northeast Asia, and they are parties to the six-party talks on the nuclear issue of the Korean Peninsula.

A Few Concluding Remarks

The Korean Peninsula developments will largely define the future of Northeast Asia, the entire Asia Pacific, and the global situation as well. I will dwell on two principal points.

On the one hand, a denuclearized Korean Peninsula would create a vital precedent for resolving similar issues in other regions and it would therefore contribute greatly to supporting the non-proliferation regime.

On the other hand, under the current global circumstances, the six-party talks are a crucial example of attempts at a collective resolution of one of the most pressing international issues. This is the only way to proceed. No unilateral pressure, no attempts to monopolize conflict resolution could stabilize an unbalanced system and contribute to its de-ideologization and demilitarization.

The Korean Peninsula is part of Northeast Asia, a multi-polar region where huge achievements and grand prospects are combined with a significant conflict potential, where tensions are ripe in finances, in the military, and in the environmental situations, where territorial claims are still unsettled. Five of the world's ten largest armies are in this region. Four states have nuclear weapons. Three more can go nuclear any time.

The two Koreas' confrontation is not the only source of Northeast Asia's military dangers. Security interests of such great powers as Russia, the US, China, and Japan overlap in the region. Under the 1953 US-South Korea Mutual Defense Treaty, South Korea is a military ally of the US. Article III of the Treaty states that "each Party recognizes that an armed attack in the Pacific area on either of the Parties in territories now under their respective administrative control, or hereafter recognized by one of the Parties as lawfully brought under the administrative control of the other, would be dangerous to its own peace and safety and declares that it would act to meet the common danger in accordance with its constitutional processes," while under article IV, "the Republic of Korea grants, and the United States of America accepts, the right to dispose United States land, air and sea forces in and about the territory of the Republic of Korea as determined by mutual agreement."

Seoul needs the American military presence to protect its economic prosperity from attempts by Pyongyang. For Washington, it is but one component of securing the US "global leadership." The Korean Peninsula is the only mainland stronghold the US has in East Asia. Besides, as an American ally in Asia Pacific, South Korea is augmenting the US military power to a far greater degree than does Japan.

Russia and South Korea maintain good neighborly relations. Russia-South Korea relations aren't marred by any contentious issues. The two countries' cooperation covers virtually every aspect of human life, from applied medicine to space exploration. There are no South Korean parties or organizations proclaiming anti-Russian slogans. South Korea has a sort of a national consensus as regards its relations with Russia, opting for strategic partnership, which provides good foundations for the two countries' relations with other states in assuring multilateral peace and security in Northeast Asia.

This task is clearly topical today. Northeast Asia is the world's only region which doesn't have a multi-lateral mechanism in place for tackling various issues of common interest, and for resolving conflicts between regional participants. Its current security architecture was shaped during the Cold War and the time of American-Soviet confrontation. It is suitable neither to the current force structure design in the Asia Pacific Region, nor to the tasks of fighting regional and global threats, and therefore, this architecture has to be radically revised.

Where to begin and how to proceed? President Park Geun-hye of the Republic of Korea proposed the peace and cooperation initiative in Northeast Asia, suggesting as its starting points the softer subjects for multilateral talks, such as environmental issues, natural disaster alleviation aid, nuclear safety code, and counter-terrorism. Such processes are supposed to enhance trust and to allow gradual transition to a wide range of subjects related to peace and development in the region.

It would probably be useful to add the issue of energy security. Despite the military and political differences between the states, all the countries in the region are united by their concern for their energy security. By 2020, over 50 per cent of global demand for energy will come from Northeast Asia. 55 per cent of Chinese oil consumption is covered by import. In Japan, it is 90 per cent. South Korea produces no oil at all.

Recently, new and sensitive shifts took place affecting the energy situation in Northeast Asia, prompted by the exacerbated global financial instability, political upheavals in the Middle East and North Africa, the Fukushima nuclear power plant disaster. Resolving these issues takes joint efforts.

Russia is definitely capable of contributing to the successful resolution of the joint task of ensuring energy security in Northeast Asia, as exemplified by the energy dialog in Russia-

South Korea economic relations. Recently, South Korean companies received billion-dollar orders for manufacturing equipment for Russia's energy projects and for state-of-the-art tankers for transporting oil and liquefied gas. Such energy projects as the Eastern Siberia–Pacific Ocean oil pipeline and Sakhalin oil and gas projects designed with South Korea and other countries of Northeast Asia in mind. Russia actively cooperates with South Korea, China and Japan in the promotion of safe nuclear power use.

The list could be expanded to include the so-called "Asian Super-Ring" aimed at integrating the energy systems of Russia, China, Mongolia, South Korea, and Japan, with Siberian and Far Eastern power plants being the principal donors, and Russia being the hub for daily power flow between countries. The project was proposed back in 1998 and it still awaits implementation.

Other projects to be included in the list is the tidal power plant in the Tugur Bay of the Sea of Okhotsk with the capacity of 8,000 mega watts. Construction of the Tugur Bay Tidal Power Plant, a radically new, environmentally safe power plant using sustainable tidal energy as its "fuel" would be an global-scale energy breakthrough.

Northeast Asian countries' joint long-term projects could be also founded on Russian initiatives for improving Eurasian transportation corridors and routes by modernizing the Trans-Siberian and Baikal-Amur mainlines and Russia's Pacific ports and also by developing new seaways, including the Northern Sea Route in addition to the congested routes via the Suez and Panama Canals.

However, these initiatives will relieve the tension in the region only if they involve all the countries in the region, including North Korea. And no special conditions should be set for Pyongyang as a pre-requisite for admitting North Korea to the

Northeast Asia club, such as, for instance, North Korea's complete and utter nuclear disarmament.

North Korea's missile launches and nuclear tests should be unequivocally condemned, yet Pyongyang should be actively involved into political dialog and joint economic projects. North Korea emerging from its isolation, its socioeconomic development, becoming a full member of international dialog would be a great asset for the world at large and for Northeast Asia and Asia Pacific. North Korea is a member of the UN and other international forums, it is recognized by nearly the entire international community.

Other countries should also exhibit restraint and common sense when implementing the UN Security Council's resolutions on the nuclear issue of the Korean Peninsula. There should be no room for unjustifiably expansive interpretation of the sanctions stipulated in those resolutions. The policy of Pyongyang's *de-facto* total international isolation would cause nothing but harm. Certain parties' expectations of the imminent collapse of the North Korean state governance are hardly justified. North Korea's system has proven its significant resilience. A North Korea which is relatively secure and self-confident would make a far better partner for any negotiations, than a cornered country burdened with sanctions.

I see reasons for optimism in the fact that a similar point of view is shared by some very influential South Koreans. I will quote Lee Hong-koo, former Prime Minister, who wrote in JoongAng Ilbo on April 22, 2013 that "durable peace on the Korean peninsula and its denuclearization would be feasible if the two Koreas establish a new framework for coexistence and co-prosperity with guarantees by the United States, China, Japan and Russia. The new framework would be most effective if the concerned parties render all available diplomatic, security and